Output-Based Aid

Output-Based Aid

Lessons Learned and Best Practices

Yogita Mumssen,
Lars Johannes, and
Geeta Kumar

THE WORLD BANK
Washington, D.C.

1818 H Street NW
Washington DC 20433
Telephone: 202-473-1000
Internet: www.worldbank.org
E-mail: feedback@worldbank.org

1 2 3 4 13 12 11 10

This volume is a product of the staff of the International Bank for Reconstruction and Development / The World Bank. The findings, interpretations, and conclusions expressed in this volume do not necessarily reflect the views of the Executive Directors of The World Bank or the governments they represent.

The World Bank does not guarantee the accuracy of the data included in this work. The boundaries, colors, denominations, and other information shown on any map in this work do not imply any judgement on the part of The World Bank concerning the legal status of any territory or the endorsement or acceptance of such boundaries.

Rights and Permissions

ISBN-13: 978-0-8213-8188-5
eISBN: 978-0-8213-8189-2
DOI: 10.1596/978-0-8213-8188-5

Library of Congress Cataloging-in-Publication Data

Mumssen, Yogita, 1970-
Output-based aid : lessons learned and best practices / Yogita Mumssen, Lars Johannes, Geeta Kumar.
      p. cm.
   Includes bibliographical references and index.
   ISBN 978-0-8213-8188-5 — ISBN 978-0-8213-8189-2 (electronic)
   1. Municipal finance—Developing countries. 2. Infrastructure (Economics)—Developing countries—Finance. 3. Municipal services—Developing countries—Finance. 4. Economic development projects—Developing countries. 5. Economic assistance—Developing countries. I. Johannes, Lars, 1976- II. Kumar, Geeta, 1977- III. World Bank. IV. Title.
   HJ9695.M88 2010
   338.9109172'4—dc22

                                                                                         2009052112

Cover design by Quantum Think
Cover photo courtesy of Global Partnership on Output-Based Aid

Contents

Boxes

Figures

Tables

Foreword

As the development community strives to improve results and aid effectiveness, the priority remains to design innovative financial solutions that meet developing countries' needs and use public funding efficiently. Results-based financing (RBF) mechanisms, which link payments to performance, are an important part of this effort. I am pleased to introduce this new report, which gives the fullest picture yet of the breadth and impact of one of the key results-based approaches, output-based aid, or OBA.

In my visits to developing countries, I have seen firsthand how access to basic services such as electricity or clean water can change peoples' lives. OBA uses performance-based subsidies to improve delivery of such services to low-income households. For me, one of OBA's main advantages is that it helps make services affordable for poor customers while at the same time giving service providers an incentive to serve them. Furthermore, given that disbursement of funds in OBA schemes mainly takes place after independent verification of outputs, such as access to electricity, donors are able to monitor where their money has gone and the results achieved.

Since OBA was first launched in the World Bank Group in 2002–03, such schemes have increased significantly, from 32 projects to nearly 200 worldwide, with various sources of funding, and they are expected to benefit at least 60 million poor people. The OBA schemes provide important lessons for the further development of RBF. The increase in OBA schemes is an indication that the approach has found its place in the spectrum of results-based instruments available to donors and governments.

OBA projects are delivering a range of essential services, from improved water supply to electricity access, reproductive health services, roads, telephone and Internet access, and education. OBA is also encouraging service providers to improve operational efficiency and provide innovative service solutions. For instance, a scheme in Nepal is subsidizing approximately 37,300 biogas plants for rural households to increase access to clean and affordable energy for cooking and lighting. Another project in Kenya is combining OBA with microfinance to enable small community-based water providers in 55 communities to connect poor households to water services. This book contains many other examples.

The authors also identify some cross-cutting challenges in implementing OBA approaches. For instance, one of OBA's purported advantages is that it shifts performance risk to service providers by paying them only after delivery of services. In some OBA schemes, however, the service providers—especially if they are small and local—find obtaining access to the finance they need to "prefinance" the agreed outputs difficult. Other financial instruments, such as guarantees, may be needed to mitigate this constraint.

The numerous pilots have provided valuable lessons on the design of OBA schemes. One challenge when scaling up pilots is to ensure that the enabling environment in terms of the regulatory and legal framework is supportive of larger OBA programs.

This review of OBA was undertaken jointly by the World Bank Group's IDA/IFC Secretariat and the Global Partnership on Output-Based Aid (GPOBA), a global partnership program administered by the World Bank. I would like to thank GPOBA's donors—Australia, the European Union, the Netherlands, Sweden, the United Kingdom, and the International Finance Corporation—for their support.

The World Bank Group has a key role to play in demonstrating that RBF approaches can improve results and aid effectiveness. I look forward to working closely with GPOBA, the IDA/IFC Secretariat, and other development partners to ensure that the lessons learned from the OBA pilots will be incorporated more frequently into the design of development projects.

Katherine Sierra
Vice President, Sustainable Development
World Bank

Acknowledgments

The review work was a collaborative effort between the Global Partnership on Output-Based Aid (GPOBA) and the IDA-IFC Secretariat. The authors would especially like to acknowledge the core team, which included Catherine Russell, Daniel Coila, Inga Murariu, Luisa Mimmi, Mark Njore, Vyjayanti Desai, and Chloe Oliver. The work was conducted under the supervision of GPOBA Program Manager Patricia Veevers-Carter, IDA-IFC Secretariat Director Nigel Twose, and Finance Economics and Urban Department Director Zoubida Allaoua.

Special thanks is extended to the peer reviewers: Amie Batson, Andreas Schliessler, Dana Rysankova, Juan-Navas Sabater, Logan Brenzel, and Luiz Claudio Martins Tavares.

Additional comments and contributions were provided by the following OBA practitioners and sector experts: Carmen Nonay, Cledan Mandri-Perrott, Dirk Sommer, Esther Loening, Iain Menzies, Juliana Guaqueta, Luis Tineo, Martin Schmid, Mustafa Hussain, and Xavier Chauvot de Beauchêne.

Comments and guidance were provided by the OBA Advisory Committee that met in February 2009, comprising Alejandro Jadresic, Irving Kuczynski, Adriana Aguinaga, Amie Batson, Doyle Gallegos, Gaiv Tata, Hartwig Schafer, Magda Lovei, Marc Juhel, Neil Gregory, Penelope Brook, Tjaarda Storm Van Leeuwen, and Vijay Jagannathan.

Abbreviations

CCT	conditional cash transfer
COD	cash on delivery
CREMA	Contrato de Recuperación y Mantenimiento (Contract for Rehabilitation and Maintenance; Argentina)
DFID	Department for International Development (U.K.)
DGIS	Directorate-General for International Cooperation (Netherlands)
DRC	Democratic Republic of Congo
ESCO	Energy Service Company
FDT	Fondo de Desarrollo de las Telecomunicaciones (Telecommunications Development Fund; Chile)
FITEL	Fondo de Inversiones en Telecomunicaciones (Fund for Telecommunications Investment; Peru)
FONDETEL	Fondo para el Desarrollo de la Telefonía (Fund for Telephony Development; Guatemala)
FSSAP	Female Secondary School Assistance Project (Bangladesh)
GEF	Global Environment Facility
GPOBA	Global Partnership on Output-Based Aid
GTZ	German Agency for Technical Cooperation

IBRD	International Bank for Reconstruction and Development
ICR	Implementation Completion and Results Report
ICT	information and communication technology
IDA	International Development Association
IDCOL	Infrastructure Development Company Limited
IDTR	Infraestructura Decentralizada para la Transformación Rural (Decentralized Infrastructure for Rural Transformation; Bolivia)
IFC	International Finance Corporation
KfW	Kreditanstalt für Wiederaufbau
MCHIP	Maternal and Child Health Insurance Program (Argentina)
M&E	monitoring and evaluation
MFI	microfinance institution
MSC	medium-term service contract
MWC	Manila Water Company
NGO	nongovernmental organization
NHAI	National Highways Authority of India
OBA	output-based aid
OECD	Organisation for Economic Co-operation and Development
ONE	Office National de l'Electricité (Morocco)
PALYJA	PT Pam Lyonnaise Jaya (Indonesia)
PBC	performance-based contracting
PER	Plan de Electrificación Rural (Rural Electrification Plan; Guatemala)
PERMER	Proyecto de Energía Renovable en el Mercado Eléctrico Rural (Renewable Energies in the Rural Market Project; Argentina)
PERZA	Proyecto de Electrificación Rural en Zonas Aisladas (Offgrid Rural Electrification Project; Nicaragua)
PPER	Rural Electrification Priority Program (Senegal)
PPP	public-private partnership
PV	photovoltaic
RBF	results-based financing
REF	Rural Electrification Fund
RERED	Rural Electrification and Renewable Energy Development
SHS	solar home system
SPUG	small power utility group
UAF	universal access fund
UASF	universal access and service fund
USF	universal service fund
WBG	World Bank Group

## PART I

Introduction to Output-Based Aid

## CHAPTER 1

Output-Based Aid: Improving Access to Basic Services for the Poor

Governments in developing countries and members of the development aid community are acutely aware of the need to find more effective ways to improve basic living conditions for the poor. Traditional approaches to delivering public support have not always led to the results intended. Results-based financing instruments are now recognized as one important piece of the aid-delivery puzzle. *Results-based financing* (RBF) is an umbrella term that includes output-based aid, provider payment incentives, performance-based interfiscal transfers, and conditional cash transfers. What these mechanisms have in common is that a principal entity provides a financial or in-kind reward, conditional on the recipient of that reward undertaking a set of predetermined actions or achieving a predetermined performance goal.[1] The ultimate aim is to increase the effectiveness of scarce public resources for the provision of basic services.

Figure 1.1 provides a broad depiction of the instruments that may be categorized as RBF approaches (although this figure is not exhaustive). RBF instruments that are not considered output based-aid (OBA) are, for example, conditional cash transfers and possibly cash on delivery, both of which are discussed in more detail in chapters 7 and 8 on the health and education sectors.

Figure 1.1   Examples of Results-Based Financing Approaches

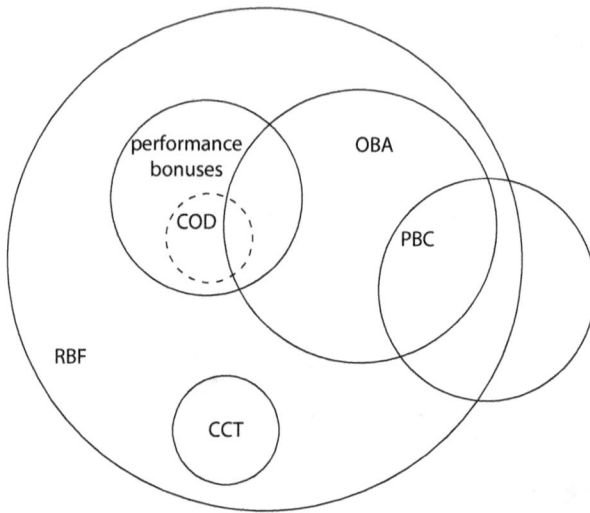

Source: Authors' representation.
Note: CCT = conditional cash transfer; COD = cash on delivery; OBA = output-based aid; PBC = performance-based contracting (for example, for roads).

Defining Output-Based Aid

Output-based aid is a results-based mechanism that is increasingly being used to deliver basic infrastructure and social services to the poor. The concept was introduced in the World Bank Group in 2002 through the Private Sector Development Strategy and more formally in January 2003. At that time, the Global Partnership on Output-Based Aid (GPOBA) was launched as a World Bank–administered donor-funded pilot program to test the approach with a view to mainstreaming OBA within the International Development Association—the World Bank arm responsible for lending to the poorest countries—as well as with other development partners.

OBA ties the disbursement of public funding in the form of subsidies to the achievement of clearly specified results that directly support improved access to basic services. *Basic services* include improved water supply and sanitation, access to energy, health care, education, communications services, and transportation.

In the case of OBA, outputs are defined as closely to the desired outcome or impact as is contractually feasible. For example, an output might be the installation of a functioning household connection to the electricity network. In some cases, an output might also include a specified period of electricity delivery demonstrated through billing and collection records. The intended outcome of such an output-based scheme would be, for example, to reduce indoor air pollution or increase opportunities for education through better lighting. The intended development impact could include, for example, a reduction in morbidity or increased lifetime earnings.

Subsidies are defined as public funding used to fill the gap between the total cost of providing a service to a user and the user fees charged for that service.[2] Policy concerns such as improving basic living conditions for the poor or reducing disease may justify the use of subsidies. Both the definition of outputs and the design of subsidy mechanisms are discussed in detail later in this book.

Neither performance arrangements nor subsidies are new. Performance contracts have been implemented for several decades, using both public and private operators. However, outputs in OBA schemes are generally more narrowly defined than benchmarks in traditional performance arrangements, which in some cases may be more input oriented. Subsidies have also existed in the infrastructure and social service sectors. OBA refines the targeting of subsidies by bringing them together with performance-based arrangements through the explicit linking of subsidy disbursement to the

Figure 1.2   Contrast of a Traditional Input-Based Approach to an Output-Based Approach

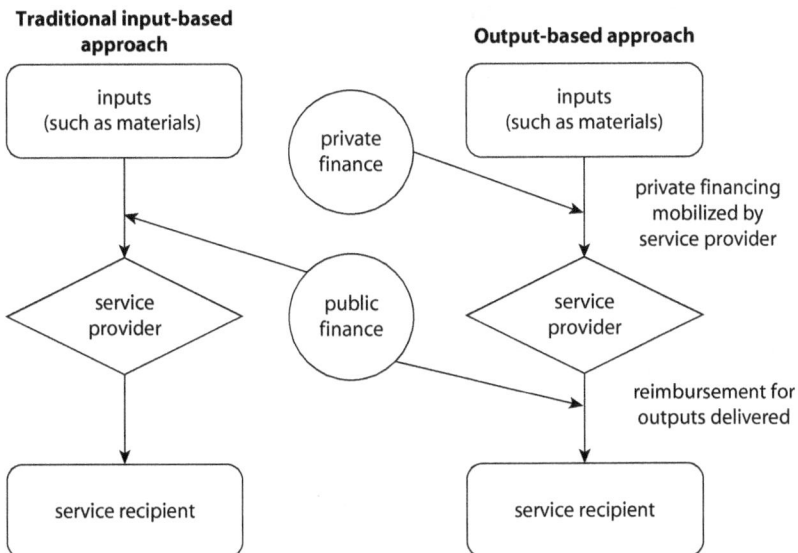

Source: Brook and Petrie 2001.

achievement of agreed outputs. Figure 1.2 provides a simple contrast of a traditional input-based approach to an output-based approach.

Another way of looking at how OBA differs from input-based approaches is to analyze the contracting spectrum often seen in infrastructure and social service delivery. Since the 1990s, schemes that harness private financing to deliver infrastructure services have expanded considerably. Under traditional procurement, private infrastructure services are contracted at the "input" end of the spectrum: the government purchases specific "inputs" and uses them to build assets and provide services itself (see figure 1.3). Under OBA schemes, services are contracted to a third-party provider, and that contract or other official arrangement is the mechanism through which the output-based disbursement criteria are established. The third party in OBA schemes is typically a private enterprise but could also be a public utility, a nongovernmental organization, a community-based organization, or even a government branch or institution separate from the entity providing the official public funds.

Contracting "closer to the input end" of the spectrum (for example, the laying of a distribution network) is several steps away from attaining the outcomes and impacts the government actually wants (for example, a reduction in waterbourne diseases and decreased morbidity, respectively). But because outcomes and impacts are a combined product of (a) what the provider can influence and (b) other factors outside the service provider's control, either governments seeking to pay on outcomes and impacts will not find a willing and credible service provider or the provider will charge a substantial premium for making its receipt of payment contingent on factors that it cannot control.

Figure 1.3   Contracting Spectrum

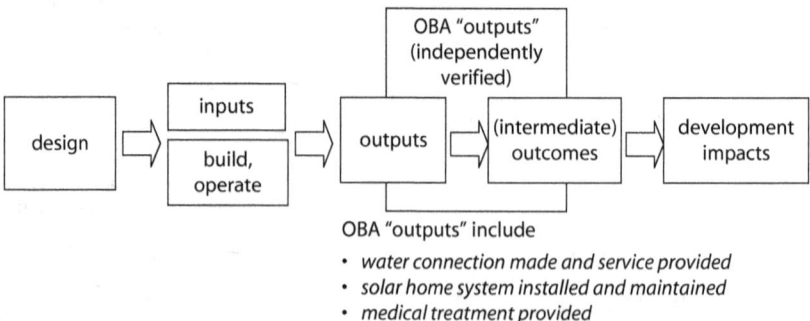

OBA "outputs" include
- *water connection made and service provided*
- *solar home system installed and maintained*
- *medical treatment provided*

Source: Authors' representation.

Nevertheless, governments can contract for an output related as closely as possible to the desired development outcome or impact, while leaving performance risk still largely under the service provider's control. This is the rationale behind *output*-based aid. Outputs would include, for example, contracting for installation of functioning yard taps as part of a water supply program, for vaccination of a specified number of people in the case of health programs, or for installation of working public pay phones or solar home systems in villages in the case of information and communication technology (ICT) or energy programs. To ensure sustainability and that service providers take on appropriate demand risk, OBA can also involve some element of payment on intermediate outcomes—for example, disbursing a portion of payments (subsidies) on the actual use of electricity or ICT services. However, the further one goes along the output-outcome-impact spectrum, the greater the risk the service provider bears. Therefore, consideration must be given to whether the provider is reasonably able to bear that risk—and at what cost.

This Book: Analyzing the Performance of OBA

The objective of this book is to provide a more definitive and practical understanding of lessons and best practices related to OBA for increased effectiveness of public spending (including donor funds) to improve access to basic services. The guiding principles are to better articulate the lessons learned from the various applications of OBA and best practices by sector. To this end, the universe of OBA projects (including projects funded outside GPOBA and the World Bank Group) was identified. Information was gathered on project design, implementation, and results, and sector-specific lessons learned and best practices of OBA. Lessons from the various applications of OBA, such as one-off subsidies, transitional subsidies, and ongoing subsidies (defined in chapter 2), were compiled.[3]

The criteria and benchmarks against which the OBA portfolio is analyzed in this book are the same criteria and benchmarks that were postulated when OBA was launched in 2002. Namely, because of the link between preidentified outputs and ex post payment ("subsidies"), the following advantages of OBA over traditional approaches were assumed:

- *Increased transparency through the explicit targeting of subsidies,* tying these subsidies to defined outputs

- *Increased accountability by shifting performance risk to service providers* by paying them only after they have delivered an agreed output
- *Increased engagement of private sector capital and expertise* by encouraging the private sector to serve customers (usually the poor) they might otherwise disregard
- *Encouragement of innovation and efficiency* by leaving the service "solutions" partly up to the service provider and through least-cost determination of subsidy required
- *Increased sustainability of public funding* by using one-off subsidies and linking ongoing subsidies to sustainable service
- *Enhancement of monitoring* of results because payments are made against agreed outputs

Table 1.1 summarizes the cross-cutting lessons in relation to best practices and challenges. These lessons were gleaned from the 197 Bank and non-Bank OBA projects reviewed. Most of the lessons are taken from projects that have closed or that are being implemented, but in some cases, important and interesting lessons could be learned from projects at the design stage. These lessons are explored in the following chapters, which consider how OBA can be applied in different contexts and how the use of OBA mechanisms can be improved.

This book is structured as follows:

- Part I includes chapter 1, which defines OBA and puts it in the context of traditional aid-delivery mechanisms and RBF instruments. Chapter 2 provides an overview of where OBA approaches are being implemented as well as a description of the various applications of OBA: one-off, transitional, or ongoing subsidies.
- Part II consists of six chapters comprising the specific sector reviews: ICT, roads (transportation), energy, water and sanitation, health, and education.
- Part III starts with chapter 9, which summarizes the lessons learned from the specific sectors, focusing on cross-cutting issues. Chapter 10 concludes the review and considers where OBA is heading and what can be done to make OBA more effective and widespread, where applicable, to help improve access to basic services for the poor.
- The appendix presents a table of all OBA projects identified in the World Bank Group to date.

Table 1.1 Benchmarks and Criteria and Cross-Cutting Lessons from OBA Portfolio

Benchmarks and criteria	Cross-cutting lessons from OBA portfolio
Increased transparency through the explicit targeting of subsidies	OBA provides a good platform for targeting infrastructure and social services subsidies. The focus on subsidies for access is inherently pro-poor: the poorest segments of the population often cannot afford initial access (for example, cost of connection, health insurance) and therefore often do not benefit from subsidies for ongoing service provision. Furthermore, if outputs are explicitly defined, targeting can be made more precise. The process of output verification can also provide an additional check on the targeting of subsidies and is helping provide early evidence that OBA schemes are reaching the poor.[a]
Increased accountability by shifting performance risk to service providers	Compared to similar input-based schemes, OBA shifts performance risk to service providers by paying providers only after delivery of verifiable access and service. However, the degree of performance risk shifted depends on the ability of the service provider to "prefinance" investments and services until output-based payments are disbursed. Ultimately, access to finance will determine how much performance risk is reasonably shifted to the provider.
Increased engagement of private sector capital and expertise	OBA does leverage private funding, but because of its generally pro-poor nature, private financing leveraged is limited by the extent that user fees (for example, tariffs) can incorporate investment costs while remaining affordable. Particularly noteworthy are the examples where, through relatively small amounts of OBA subsidy, private sector expertise can be mobilized to extend services to customer segments the private sector might otherwise not reach. Ultimately, the effective use of private sector participation depends on the enabling environment—for example, the depth and quality of experience with public-private partnership contracts, regulation, and access to finance.
Encouragement of innovation and efficiency	Some evidence indicates that output-based payments have led to improvements in operational efficiency and the delivery of innovative, often pro-poor, access-to-service solutions. Moreover, OBA has demonstrated efficiency gains through competition in most sectors when competitive pressures have been applied in the selection of the OBA service provider (although competitive tendering processes can take time). The focus on outputs rather than inputs should lead to innovations that translate into future efficiency gains, as has been seen in ICT and to some extent in roads.

(continued)

9

Table 1.1 Benchmarks and Criteria and Cross-Cutting Lessons from OBA Portfolio (*Continued*)

Benchmarks and criteria	Cross-cutting lessons from OBA portfolio
Increased sustainability of public funding	It is too early to analyze whether OBA schemes have provided long-term sustainable solutions. No evidence to date suggests that schemes involving OBA subsidies are less sustainable than their input-based counterparts. In fact, the design of OBA schemes—for example, greater degree of demand risk shifted to service providers given the link between outputs and uptake, which in turn incentivizes efforts at stakeholder participation and education through community organizations, nongovernmental organizations, and the like—can enhance longer-term sustainability.
Enhancement of monitoring of results	By paying on verified outputs, OBA internalizes the monitoring of results. Best practice would also use the monitoring platform of OBA beyond just the verification of outputs to check other aspects of service delivery. With OBA schemes, accountability also increases for donors and governments: public funding is linked to delivery of preidentified outputs, and therefore waste or inappropriate allocation of such funding should be minimized.

Source: Authors' summary.

a. Explicit targeting of subsidies for specific users and uses is common across all the sectors where OBA is prevalent, except for the road sector (and to a limited extent ICT), where the "public good" (access for all) nature makes exclusively targeting specific beneficiaries difficult.

Notes

1. See, for example, World Bank 2008c. Some of these RBF instruments are described in more detail in the health and education chapters, where the most varied array of RBF instruments is being tested to date.

2. In some cases—for example, public goods such as roads—user fees may be zero.

3. Much of the work has been conducted in house by the GPOBA monitoring and evaluation team, which is tasked with documenting and disseminating lessons learned—both best practices and challenges—from OBA schemes in and outside the World Bank Group. Castalia consultants provided some support on the ICT and road sectors.

## CHAPTER 2

Snapshot of the OBA Universe

This review has identified that approximately 32 output-based aid (OBA) projects existed at the time of the official launch of OBA in 2002–03, totaling US$1.5 billion in funding.[1] Now, about 131 OBA projects with a total value of about US$3.5 billion in subsidies (excluding the US$2.8 billion subsidy funded by recipient governments) have been identified in the World Bank Group (WBG; figure 2.1).[2]

Another 66 OBA schemes have been identified outside the WBG, mostly in the information and communication technology (ICT), transport (mainly roads), and energy sectors (predominantly in Latin America and Africa). Additional OBA schemes may exist that this review did not discover.

Most WBG OBA projects are in Latin America and the Caribbean, where the first OBA pilots in almost each sector were initiated, as well as in Africa, partly because of piloting efforts in that region by GPOBA. By number of projects the WBG OBA portfolio is spread evenly across the sectors, except for only a handful of education projects identified. However, the total WBG subsidy may present a different picture, for example, the subsidy percent attributable to ICT is small (Figure 2.1b) despite the pervasiveness of OBA in the sector. This is largely because a large part of the subsidy in ICT is not donor

Figure 2.1   Volume of OBA Subsidy by Sector and Region in the WBG

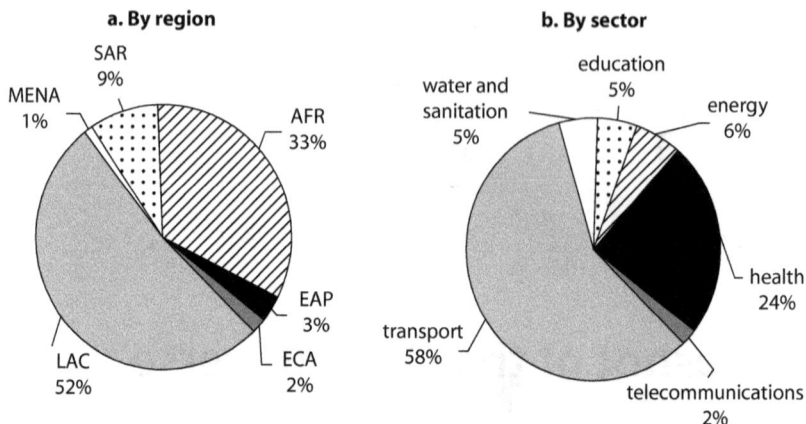

a. By region

SAR
9%

MENA
1%

AFR
33%

EAP
3%

ECA
2%

LAC
52%

b. By sector

education
5%

water and
sanitation
5%

energy
6%

health
24%

transport
58%

telecommunications
2%

Source: GPOBA database.
Note: Total subsidy = US$3.5 billion. AFR = Sub-Saharan Africa Region; EAP = East Asia and Pacific Region; ECA = Europe and Central Asia Region; LAC = Latin America and Caribbean Region; MENA = Middle East and North Africa Region; SAR = South Asia Region.

funded, but generated from license fees and levies from within the sector itself (see Chapter 3 on ICT).

Of the projects identified in the WBG, 34 are closed, 78 are under implementation and for the most part delivering outputs, and 19 are in design stage. This review draws mostly from the closed projects and those under implementation, although some important lessons can be learned from project design.

The nearly fourfold increase in the number of OBA projects in the WBG within a period of five years is most likely caused by a variety of factors, including the following:

- An increased emphasis on results and accountability by donors and governments, including the WBG results agenda
- An explicit recognition that well-designed subsidy schemes are an integral part of a pro-poor infrastructure and social services delivery strategy
- A recognition that for private-public partnerships to be successful, specific attention needs to be paid to pro-poor service delivery

This explicit acknowledgment that subsidies are sometimes necessary, coupled with new evidence that many existing subsidy schemes such as quantity-based subsidies embedded in tariffs often have a regressive targeting incidence (Komives and others 2005), has contributed to the appeal of more targeted subsidy schemes such as OBA.

Although the OBA portfolio has been growing substantially, to put this growth in context, at about 3 percent in total, OBA is only a small share of the World Bank portfolio. The largest share of OBA projects was 9.1 percent of funding volume in the ICT sector, followed by health (7.1 percent) and transport (3.6 percent).

In addition to OBA's not yet fully mainstreamed status, several factors contribute to this low percentage. Whereas the WBG's OBA portfolio includes only projects that aim at increasing household access to basic services, the overall portfolio includes projects financing large upstream investments, wider sector-reform programs, and analytic and advisory activities. Moreover, the overall WBG portfolio obtained from the WBG Business Warehouse database includes subsectors such as mining, railways, ports, and nutrition—for which no OBA projects have been identified.

Preliminary Evidence on the Effectiveness of OBA

OBA projects are delivering results:

- The 89 projects for which data are available[3] are expected to reach 61 million planned beneficiaries.
- So far, 17.4 million people are verified to have benefited from OBA projects.
- The closed projects for which information is available have reached 16 percent more beneficiaries than planned.
- In OBA, transport projects have rehabilitated and maintained 87,591 kilometers of roads or are in the process of doing so.

Development outcome ratings obtained from World Bank Implementation Completion Reports (ICRs) provide some evidence that the OBA projects reviewed have been more effective in achieving development outcomes than traditional projects (figure 2.2). This finding is based on the ratings of all OBA ICRs available compared with all ICRs submitted in OBA sectors in fiscal year 2007. Both in the overall outcome ratings of the ICRs and the Bank's Independent Evaluation Group outcome ratings, OBA projects score on average half a category higher than traditional

Figure 2.2   Comparison of ICR Overall Outcome Ratings

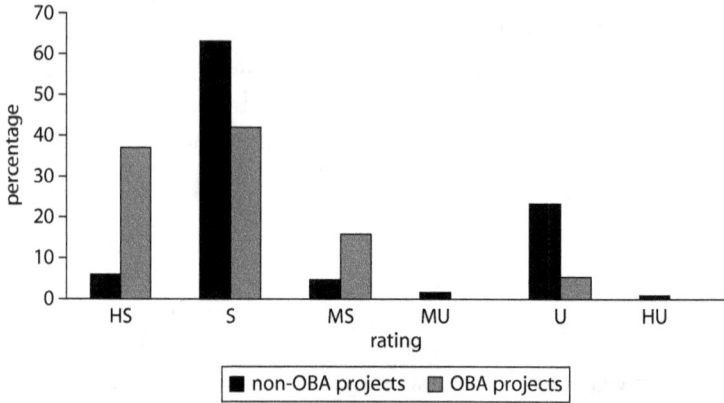

Source: GPOBA database.

Note: HS = highly satisfactory; S = satisfactory; MS = moderately satisfactory; MU = moderately unsatisfactory; U = unsatisfactory; HU = highly unsatisfactory.

projects. Results are similar for ratings of the quality at entry and quality of supervision of projects that is assessed by the World Bank's Independent Evaluation Unit. For OBA projects, quality at entry is rated highly successful or successful in 77 percent of cases, and quality of entry is rated highly successful or successful in 100 percent of cases.

Additional evidence on the relative effectiveness of OBA in relation to the OBA benchmarks and criteria is discussed in part II of this book, including data supporting the case that transferring performance risk has led to a reduction in cost overruns and benefit shortfalls in OBA projects compared to traditional aid approaches.

Where Does the Funding Come From?

Funding for OBA schemes has come from the International Bank for Reconstruction and Development (IBRD), the International Development Association (IDA), GPOBA, other donors such as the German development bank KfW (Kreditanstalt für Wiederaufbau), and governments themselves using, for example, tax revenues and cross-subsidies collected from users. IDA and IBRD are the biggest donors with over US$3.3 billion committed to fund subsidies to 80 projects.[4] Many of the first projects were in the Latin American region and in the roads and ICT sectors. Subsequent roads and ICT schemes have built on the lessons from these schemes (with varying degrees of success) and expanded into other regions so that a substantial number of roads and ICT schemes now exist in regions such as Sub-Saharan Africa.

Projects in IBRD countries tend to be larger than those in IDA countries, with the 29 percent of projects located in IBRD countries accounting for more than half of OBA subsidies. A number of projects have also received substantial amounts of complementary subsidy funding from the recipient governments worth a total of US$2.8 billion.[5] Nearly 8 of every 10 dollars of this complementary funding came from IBRD governments. The bulk of this government funding has been in the transport and health sectors, accounting together for 88 percent of funding.

The remaining 51 projects of the WBG portfolio either have received funding or are in the process of being funded by GPOBA. GPOBA is a World Bank–administered program created in 2003 by the United Kingdom's Department for International Development (DFID) and the World Bank. GPOBA was originally intended to help assist in preparing OBA projects and to document and disseminate the lessons learned. In 2005, through an additional DFID contribution, GPOBA became able to fund actual subsidy schemes. These funds galvanized the development of more than 40 projects, which are mostly being implemented or awaiting imminent agreements for grants. An additional 11 projects have received or are receiving GPOBA technical assistance funding. New donors have since joined GPOBA, including the Netherlands' Directorate-General for International Cooperation (DGIS), the Australian Agency for International Development (AusAid), the Swedish International Development Cooperation Agency (SIDA), and the IFC (International Finance Corporation).

GPOBA has to some extent focused on designing and developing OBA schemes in areas where OBA has been less tested, for example, in IDA countries and, in particular, the water and sanitation sector. Two-thirds of the GPOBA projects are in IDA countries, and they account for over three-quarters of GPOBA funding volume. Nearly half of GPOBA projects are in the water and sanitation sector, followed by energy. Together, these two sectors account for approximately three-quarters of GPOBA projects and funding volume. Although OBA was originally envisioned as a tool to enhance private sector participation, GPOBA has attempted to pilot OBA with commercially viable state-owned enterprises in sectors where public utilities have continued to play a dominant role in service provision.

OBA schemes were also identified outside the WBG—in both industrial and developing countries. In some cases, donors are playing an active role, such as KfW in the health and renewable energy sectors, or DGIS, through the Energizing Development program, implemented by the German Agency for Technical Cooperation in the energy sector. More generally, in developing countries, OBA schemes that do not involve donor support are mainly found in middle-income (IBRD) countries that are able to fund subsidy schemes largely from cross-subsidies or tax revenue.

Variations to OBA Applications

OBA schemes normally apply performance-based subsidies in three ways: one-off subsidies such as connection subsidies, transitional tariff subsidies that taper off as user contributions increase, or ongoing subsidies. The subsidy design chosen will depend on factors such as the sustainability of the funding source, the capacity for administering the subsidy scheme, the type of service to be subsidized, and the extent to which the service provider is willing and able to be paid over time. (See box 2.1.)

Box 2.1

Applications of OBA Subsidy Design Mechanisms

One-off subsidies are the most common application of OBA approaches and usually involve capital subsidies for access to a given service. Most OBA schemes in water, energy, and telecommunications rely on one-off subsidies enabling initial access, partly because OBA is targeted to the poor, and the poor are usually not connected to network services in the first place so often cannot benefit from ongoing or transitional tariff subsidies. Nevertheless, because in OBA approaches the emphasis is on service delivery rather than on physical connections, even in the case of one-off subsidies, a portion of the subsidy may be phased in only after verification of a certain number of months of satisfactory service delivery, thus disbursing one-off subsidies against a mixture of outputs and intermediate outcomes.

(continued)

Box 2.1 *(Continued)*

Transitional subsidies can be used to support tariff reforms, where a subsidy is used to fill the gap between what the user is deemed able or willing to pay and the cost-recovery level (for example, the long-run marginal cost) of the tariff. The subsidy is transitioned out after a specified time (for example, months or years) as the user contribution increases (and possibly as tariff levels required for cost recovery decrease with efficiency gains). In these cases, the output against which the subsidy is paid is the service delivered and billed by the provider. The review identified only a handful of transitional OBA schemes, and very few of those are still in place. One risk with such schemes would be government unwillingness to eventually increase tariffs and phase out subsidies.

Ongoing subsidies may be required in cases where a continuous gap exists between affordability and cost recovery—including for consumption costs. Ongoing output-based subsidies in the utility sectors are seen more often in countries with higher rates of access. For example, in Chile an income-based targeting scheme channels an ongoing output-based subsidy through service providers to poor urban households for a lifeline (minimum acceptable) amount of water consumed.[a] Ongoing output-based subsidies normally fund the provision of basic services or maintenance in OBA projects in roads, health, and education. OBA road maintenance schemes require ongoing subsidies for the life of the road, often funded through road funds. OBA health schemes, to ensure continued access to care for the poor, often channel subsidies in an ongoing manner through health care providers as they deliver agreed services, such as well-child visits, over a defined period.

a. Most other commonly used quantity-based tariff subsidies, such as increasing block tariffs, however, are *not* OBA. Such schemes usually charge tariffs below cost for low consumption, because poor households are assumed to consume small amounts. These subsidies are usually intended to be financed by cross-subsidies from higher-consuming customers (who are charged higher tariffs). However, the amount of cross-subsidy received by the operator is not related to the extent of service provided to the low-consuming households (i.e. the target population, supposedly poor), but rather to consumption and the subsidy collected from the high-consuming households. Therefore, the operator "earns" the subsidy from the high-consuming households whether or not it serves the targeted households.

What is clear is that for OBA or any innovative mechanism to become relevant, its application must be adaptable to regional and sector circumstances and constraints. Figure 2.3 and table 2.1 show the key sectors under review and provide the amount of subsidy of OBA projects by sector and region identified in the WBG.

Figure 2.3   Distribution of OBA Portfolio by Sector and Region

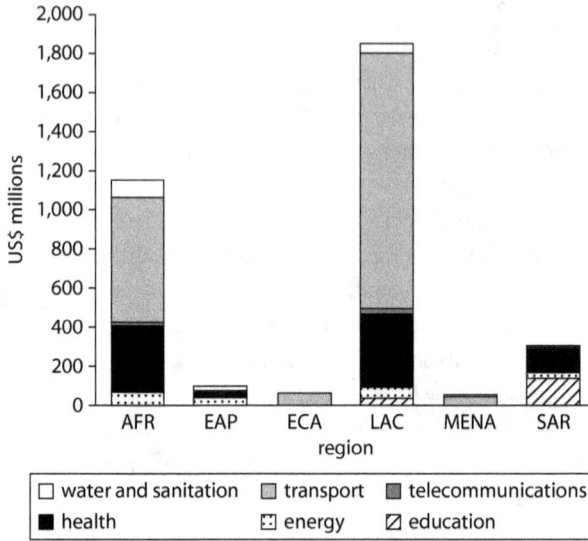

Source: GPOBA database.
Note: AFR = Sub-Saharan Africa Region; EAP = East Asia and Pacific Region; ECA = Europe and Central Asia Region; LAC = Latin America and the Caribbean Region; MENA = Middle East and North Africa Region; SAR = South Asia Region.

Because OBA approaches can vary a great deal depending on the sector context, best practices and challenges encountered are easier to delineate by sector. Part II of this book provides a more detailed description of lessons learned on a sector-by-sector basis. Cross-cutting lessons are discussed in more detail later in part III.

Table 2.1   Distribution of OBA Portfolio by Sector and Region
U.S. dollars

Region	Education	Energy	Health	Telecommunications	Transport	Water and sanitation	Total
Sub-Saharan Africa	0	68,350,000	337,301,164	21,490,705	635,588,000	89,461,433	1,152,191,302
East Asia and Pacific	3,000,000	40,600,000	26,140,000	10,076,630	0	21,525,640	101,342,270
Europe and Central Asia	0	10,100,000	0	0	55,000,000	0	65,100,000
Latin America and the Caribbean	41,140,000	52,710,000	375,104,000	29,950,000	1,303,026,000	47,380,880	1,849,310,880
Middle East and North Africa	0	0	6,232,100	0	40,000,000	8,400,000	54,632,100
South Asia	138,007,143	32,370,000	119,000,000	11,900,000	0	2,264,743	303,541,886
Total	**182,147,143**	**204,130,000**	**863,777,264**	**73,417,335**	**2,033,614,000**	**169,032,696**	**3,526,118,438**

Source: GPOBA database.

Notes

1. At the time of the Private Sector Development Strategy and the creation of the Global Partnership on Output-Based Aid, only 22 OBA projects with a total value of about US$100 million were identified, but further research has identified 11 more projects and substantially more OBA funding.

2. The figures used reflect projects identified through September 30, 2009.

3. Data on the number of beneficiaries are not readily available for public access projects that provide service to an entire population and whose use is not exclusive. Such projects are mainly found in the ICT and transport sectors.

4. This total excludes projects with GPOBA subsidy funding or technical assistance.

5. This sum does not include the approximately US$6 billion identified as collected through universal access and service funds, as discussed in chapter 3.

## PART II

OBA Review by Sector

Information and Communication Technology

Before countries liberalized their information and communication technology (ICT) sectors, public (monopoly) utilities generally had limited success in expanding ICT services. Cross-subsidy schemes were usually not successful, in part because state-owned enterprises were often unable to charge high enough tariffs to wealthier customers to help finance the price of extension to more costly, remote rural areas inhabited by the poor. Therefore, access to the poor was limited.

Since the mid-1990s, however, a substantial change has occurred in the sector. The sector went from service provision based largely on monopolies to services based on competition, which had a major impact on expanding access. During this time, output-based contracts for the provision of ICT services became an effective means of expanding those services to the poor (Stern and Townsend 2007). The first of these contracts was funded by Chile's Telecommunications Development Fund (Fondo de Desarrollo de las Telecomunicaciones; FDT) in 1995. FDT has since funded the installation of more than 25,000 public pay phones in about 8,000 rural centers, benefiting close to 2.7 million people (see box 3.1).

Other similar schemes throughout Latin America followed Chile's FDT. In 2001, Peru was the first country to develop OBA contracts for the

Box 3.1

Telecommunications Development Fund in Chile

In 1995, the government of Chile established the Telecommunications Development Fund (Fondo de Desarrollo de las Telecomunicaciones) to attract private investment in public pay phone services for rural and urban areas with low incomes and low telephone density. FDT has since funded the installation of more than 25,000 public pay phones in about 8,000 rural population centers, benefiting close to 2.7 million people. An estimated fewer than 150,000 people (1 percent of the population) now lack access to a basic phone. The subsidies awarded cost the government less than 0.3 percent of total telecommunications sector revenue during the funding period, and administering the FDT costs about 3 percent of the monies granted. Between 1995 and 2000, rural telecommunications operators invested US$161 million in universal access projects. Of this amount, FDT provided US$22 million (13.6 percent).

FDT succeeded because of a highly competitive market prior to its launch and, therefore, the ability to rely extensively on market forces to determine and allocate subsidies; less regulatory discretion; simple and relatively expeditious processing; and effective government leadership.

Competition between existing and new operators for the rural market substantially reduced the cost of phone services to the government (especially compared to earlier public sector investments in similar facilities). Some concerns remain, however, about the long-term sustainability of the services; the small, residual rural population that is still excluded; and some urban areas.

Sources: Stern and Townsend 2007: 92; Wellenius 2002.

provision of private Internet connections. The Latin America and Caribbean Region has been the forerunner in contracts for all ICT technologies. Sub-Saharan Africa implemented its first ICT output-based aid (OBA) contracts in 2002, the South Asia Region in 2004, and the East Asia and Pacific Region in 2006.

Currently, OBA is largely mainstreamed in the ICT sector, where universal access and service funds (UASFs) rely on explicit subsidies from wealthier, largely urban populations to help extend access on a performance basis to rural populations that are less wealthy and usually more costly to serve (see table 3.1). The subsidy amount is often determined by having private companies bid on the lowest subsidy required for rollout of infrastructure and services. The subsidy is disbursed on outputs, or

Table 3.1   Universe of OBA in the ICT Sector

Common output	Serviceable asset
Public phones	Provision of public phone connections (for example, Cambodia, Chile, Guatemala, India, Indonesia, Malawi, Mongolia, Nepal, Nigeria, Uganda, Zambia)
Telecenters (facilities that offer use of ICT in a publicly shared manner, with or without a fee)	Provision of telecenters (for example, Brazil, Chile, Indonesia, Mongolia)
Internet	Internet coverage through points of presence and private connections (for example, Uganda, Organization of Eastern Caribbean States)
Cellular network	Provision of cellular networks (for example, Bolivia, Mongolia)
Private phone connections	Provision of private phone connections (for example, Pakistan, Uganda)

Source: GPOBA database.

milestones—such as the installation of functioning hardware (for example, public pay phones, telecenters, or Internet points of presence)—and, in some cases, continued service provision for a specified period.

The review has identified 20 World Bank Group projects[1] and about 20 projects outside the Bank that can be considered OBA in the ICT sector. Information on contract value exists for 16 projects, which are World Bank funded and have a total value of US$73.4 million (figure 3.1). Information on the number of expected beneficiaries is available for 12 projects (total volume US$63.6 million), which are expected to reach more than 17.6 million beneficiaries. The OBA projects involve a number of different ICT services, including public pay phones; telecenters; private phone connections; Internet service, including private connections as well as wholesale facilities known as points of presence; and cellular networks. OBA for public pay phones is the most common type identified, with telecenters second, partly because of the more public—and therefore pro-poor—nature of these two services. As discussed below, however, this situation is changing.

Because of a combination of factors, the relative value of OBA projects is small, both in absolute terms (US$73 million) and compared to the World Bank ICT portfolio (9 percent of projects approved through fiscal year 2008). ICT universal access projects are mainly financed through universal access funds (UAFs) and universal service funds (USFs), referred to jointly in this book as UASFs, that usually receive their backing from sources other than development aid. As a result,

Figure 3.1   Regional Distribution of World Bank Group OBA ICT Projects

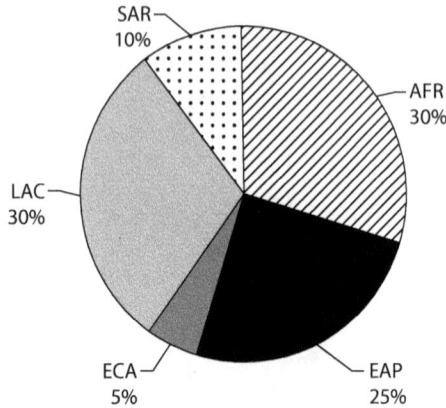

Pie chart:
- SAR 10%
- AFR 30%
- EAP 25%
- ECA 5%
- LAC 30%

Source: GPOBA database.

Note: AFR = Sub-Saharan Africa Region; EAP = East Asia and Pacific Region; ECA = Europe and Central Asia Region; LAC = Latin America and Caribbean Region; SAR = South Asia Region. Total number of projects = 20.

donors (such as the World Bank) focus on key and necessary aspects of ICT development, such as setting up regulatory regimes or financing international infrastructure to ensure interconnection.

Funding

UASFs are funded from one or a combination of the following three sources:

- *Levies on telecommunications operators.* The most common method for funding universal access and services is governments' levies on a percentage of telecommunications operators' revenues. Levies identified range between 1 and 4 percent and average about 2 percent.
- *Spectrum auctions.* Governments or sector regulators hold auctions to distribute ICT and radio spectrum to raise funding for the country's UASF (for example, Guatemala's Fund for Telephony Development [Fondo para el Desarrollo de la Telefonía; FONDETEL]).
- *Government budgets.* In a limited number of cases, governments fund the UASFs from their own budget, as is the case in Chile's FDT (see box 3.1).

The scale of subsidies varies between projects. Subsidies for the provision of public phone connections were lowest in Chile, where they averaged US$996 per phone. Such subsidies were highest in Nigeria, where they averaged US$5,511 per phone. The average subsidies per phone in projects for which information is available were US$2,848. However, subsidy values can vary greatly depending on technology. Also, a few ICT projects have recently seen "zero subsidy" required.

UASFs have been an effective mechanism for mobilizing investment into challenging rural areas. In 1994, Guatemala's FONDETEL became the first to make financing available competitively under a reverse auction (lowest subsidy demanded wins) and generate new licenses for rural operators.

Maximum subsidies to be paid by UASFs are typically calculated at the amount required to make projects commercially viable. For instance, in a project of Bolivia's telecommunications regulator Sittel, Sittel determined the maximum subsidy required to make the net present value of each public phone connection zero through projections of necessary investment and demand.

However, although the funding source in ICT OBA has become explicit and is considered sustainable, another problem has arisen: UASFs have succeeded at collecting revenue from explicit subsidy contributions, but they have *not* succeeded at disbursing it. Beginning in the late 1990s, but mainly since 2001 and 2002, 15 operational funds in developing markets collected a total of approximately US$6.2 billion from operators. Of the total collections, US$4.8 billion (78 percent) came from two countries—India and Brazil. By 2006, these 15 funds had redistributed approximately US$1.62 billion to the sector for universal access and service projects—just 26 percent of the total collected.[2] Some of the reasons given for the limited redistribution include the following (Stern and Townsend 2007):

• Defining eligible programs too narrowly by accepting only those proposals linked to public pay phones and community Internet
• Overestimating the amount of subsidy that operators would request
• Requiring that programs be approved by two or more ministries, that they must comply with all public expenditure review and monitoring procedures, or that they must conclusively demonstrate that the subsidies are well designed
• Imposing significant legal, administrative, and financial burdens that act as a barrier on operators' participation in tenders, especially for smaller operators

Alternative models that would allow for the more efficient and effective management of UASFs are being considered, such as "pay or play" or virtual funds (with no actual physical fund). Private management of

UASFs is also a possibility, such as that in the United States and a new, privately managed UASF in Pakistan. In pay or play, usually no tendering occurs; rather, obligations are allocated among the service providers. Players are free to contract with each other to fulfill their share of obligations, if paying someone else to do so makes economic sense. No country has yet established a virtual fund, but the advantage seen in virtual funds is mainly that the money from operator levies does not need to physically move into—and then later out of—a fund to the recipient, thus eliminating the need for fund management. A virtual fund would simply be an accounting system that records each operator's annual UASF levy. However, subsidy values can vary greatly depending on technology. Also, a few ICT projects have recently seen "zero subsidy" required.

Targeting

Targeting for output-based contracts for the provision of ICT access is largely geographic. Governments define target areas based on the level of telephony coverage. Some projects target smaller communities because they are likely to be areas with the least economical service provision or with a low income level. Most OBA schemes target public (shared or community) access to maximize use by the poor. However, because the nature and cost of technology is rapidly changing, private (household) access through OBA UASFs is increasing:

- Uganda's Energy for Rural Transformation project (Navas-Sabater and Ampah 2007) aims to provide at least one public phone connection per 2,500 inhabitants throughout Uganda (equating to an average of one connection about each 3 kilometers in distance). Another targeting objective is to provide rural multipurpose telecenters at schools, hospitals, and associations of farmers and microentrepreneurs outside of district capitals in selected districts. The results of the ICT component of this Energy for Rural Transformation project have, on the whole, been very successful; outputs have been delivered, and the next stages of ICT expansion in rural Uganda are under way (World Bank 2009).

- Many UASFs set national targets for telecenter coverage. In these schemes, telecenters will reach poor areas but are not targeted specifically to poor people. For example, Mexico's UAF aims to provide at least one telecenter (community digital center) per municipality in the country. Of the telecenters established to date, 71 percent have been in schools and libraries (accessible to poor people and staffed to help people learn to use the computers). Part of the telecenter program is aimed at developing local educational, health, economic, and government content (Stern and Townsend 2007).

- The Mongolia Information and Communications Infrastructure Development Project targets poor, underserved areas. It is a follow-up to the pilot funded by the Global Partnership on Output-Based Aid that has operated successfully since 2007, bringing phone service to about 20,000 beneficiaries in remote herder communities and both mobile phone and Internet services to 2,315 people in rural villages. A user survey showed that the pilot funded by the Global Partnership on Output-Based Aid has cut the distance herders must travel to reach a phone by more than half and has also more than doubled the frequency with which they use phone service (Dymond, Oestmann, and McConnell 2008: 3).

Performance Risk

Contracts for the provision of public phone connections most commonly define performance as installation of working public phone connections, with subsidies disbursed when such connections have been provided and determined to be in good working order. Some of the more effective contracts disburse a portion of subsidies upon installation of the phones and disburse the rest on a regular basis provided the phones are maintained to defined standards, as was the case in Peru's Fund for Telecommunications Investment (Fondo de Inversiones en Telecomunicaciones; FITEL), which has been largely successful. Since 2000, FITEL has increased the access to public telephony for nearly 6.7 million people, reducing the average distance to reach a public pay phone from 56 to 5.7 kilometers (Stern and Townsend 2007: 95). The economic development impact of improved coverage and access to telecommunications has been significant in Peru: the cost savings equaled 2 to 3.5 times the cost of using the FITEL phones (Stern and Townsend 2007: Executive Summary, ii).

In the 40 projects identified (both within and outside the World Bank Group), three main ways of defining performance are as follows:

- *Construction and installation completion milestones:* Contracts that define performance as construction completion milestones disburse some subsidies prior to the delivery of a serviceable asset.

- *Provision of serviceable assets:* Contracts that define performance as provision of serviceable assets disburse all subsidies at the delivery of the serviceable asset.
- *Provision of serviceable assets and continued service:* Contracts that define performance as provision of serviceable assets and continued service disburse some subsidies upon the delivery of the asset and some subsidies upon the successful continuation of service.

Table 3.2 gives examples of OBA projects that use each type of scheme for defining performance.

Also important is that although most of the contracts identified do not disburse OBA subsidies based on the provision of continued service, the contracts do include longer-term service provision requirements. These contracts are commonly in operation for 5 to 10 years. Contractors are sometimes required to post performance bonds to incentivize continuing service provision; however, most ICT companies will have other incentives to continue service provision. For example, ICT companies are sometimes granted operating licenses for up to 15 years, some of which allow the use of radio frequencies and can be revoked in the case of a breach of contract.

Table 3.2   Defining Performance in the Provision of ICT Services

Indicator	Example
Construction and installation completion milestones	In Nigeria's Privatization Support Project (Sub-Project 2), performance is defined by construction completion milestones over a 16-month period. The project's subsidy was paid in six tranches over a 16-month period. The first payment of 10 percent was paid upon contract signature and provision of certificates and guarantees. Remaining tranches were paid on the basis of installation goals.
Serviceable assets	Chile's FDT pays subsidies in a lump sum once the phones have been installed.
Serviceable assets and continued service	In contracts funded by Peru's FITEL, 40 percent of the subsidies are delivered on the basis of continued service provision over the course of five years.
	In Mongolia, the Information and Communications Infrastructure Development Project disbursed 20 percent of the subsidies on contract signature; 60 percent on realization of several output targets, such as providing service in a number of herder communities or reaching a number of mobile phone subscribers; and 20 percent after nine months of successful operation.

Source: GPOBA database.

Private Sector Capital and Expertise

In all the cases identified, private sector companies were contracted for the provision of ICT networks. Usually, government agencies or a UASF defined the area and the minimum number of people to be served. Contracted companies were able to choose the technology that would most efficiently allow the provision of coverage. Companies were also able to choose whether they would provide service beyond the target community using the infrastructure installed under the UASF contract, giving a potential for economies of scale and thereby increasing private sector incentives.

Leveraging of private sector capital varied in the identified contracts. In Guatemala's FONDETEL projects, each US$1 of subsidy leveraged between US$2 and US$4 of private investment. In Peru's FITEL projects, an average of US$2 of private capital was raised for each US$1 of subsidy. Most of the UAFs aimed to provide subsidies that would make the net present value of providing ICT services equal to zero. In other words, without subsidies, the net present value of the project would likely be less than zero and the project would not be commercially viable. The intensity of competition between bidders for ICT contracts can greatly affect the amount of private sector leveraging. For example, the Chilean telecommunications company bid 100 percent of the maximum available subsidy in localities close to its existing network where no other established local companies operated and zero subsidy in areas where its competitors had a strong presence.

OBA was originally piloted to mobilize private sector expertise to serve segments of the population that without a subsidy would most likely go unserved. For example, in Uganda, when two commercial operators declared they could not serve almost 20 percent of subcounties on a commercial basis, OBA contracts were designed to specifically target these unserved subcounties. For mitigation of demand risk under the OBA contracts, including the risk of surprise substitutes, these areas were removed from the license obligations of the non-OBA providers and awarded exclusively to the OBA providers. Because the ICT sector is very dynamic, however, instances also occur in which operators have started to provide services in areas originally thought to be noncommercial. This situation has led to the redesign of an OBA scheme in Cambodia, prior to grant signing, to ensure that only those areas that are not attractive without a subsidy fall within the OBA grant agreement.

Monitoring

As described earlier, outputs that are normally designated for OBA projects in the ICT sector include (a) construction and installation completion milestones (for example, for the rollout of network); (b) installation of serviceable assets (for example, working pay phones); and (c) completion of public access objectives and continued service (for example, provision of a working asset plus demonstration of service over a course of several months or years).

Under most contracts, except those in Chile and recently Peru, the regulatory authority for the sector manages the UASF. In some cases, the UAF performs monitoring and evaluation of the specific contracts as well.

In projects funded by Peru's FITEL, for instance, the regulator Osiptel uses a network management system to oversee system operations (traffic levels, continuity of service) in real time. Osiptel's monitoring and evaluation scheme also requires a dedicated data circuit in the operator's headquarters to monitor billing, failure reports, and the calls placed and received by the rural pay phones. In a semiannual report, Osiptel assesses compliance with performance targets and indicators and makes recommendations on FITEL payments.

Box 3.2 provides an example from Guatemala where a lack of monitoring and evaluation meant providers were not held accountable to

---

Box 3.2

Fund for Telephony Development in Guatemala

The government of Guatemala established the Fund for Telephony Development, which sought to expand the coverage of public and private phone lines to about 5,000 rural localities that represented more than half of all households without access to phone services. FONDETEL was funded by spectrum auctions. It contracted private firms for the provision of public phones in or near localities with the least access to ICT services.

Since 1998, FONDETEL has subsidized the construction of more than 5,500 public phones, benefiting about 1.49 million people. However, a World Bank–funded inspection of 220 public phones found that only 28 phones were "adequately functioning." Only 20 percent of targeted localities were estimated to have "adequate service." The study commented that FONDETEL's

(continued)

Box 3.2 *(Continued)*

methodology for selecting these underserved communities was flawed, because it did not consider cell phone coverage and usage. Disregard of these factors made urban areas with high cellular teledensity eligible for subsidized public phones.

The delivery of serviceable public phones was hampered by two factors: (a) payment was not sufficiently linked to performance, with all subsidies disbursed directly after the installation of the phones, but before a period of service was provided; and (b) nearly no monitoring and evaluation of the installation of the phones was performed.

Revisions to the FONDETEL arrangements are expected to improve the linking of payments to performance as well as enhancement of monitoring and evaluation measures.

Source: Stern and Townsend 2007: XVII, 94.

the outputs prescribed by their contract. Currently, the Bank is working with the government on new implementing measures to address some of the failures.

Notes

1. Many of these projects involve more than one contract.
2. InfoDev and International Telecommunication Union. ICT Regulation Toolkit. http://www.ictregulationtoolkit.org/en/Section.3180.html.

## CHAPTER 4

Roads

Governments and donors alike have recognized the drawbacks of in-house management of roads. Hence, for many years, they have relied on outsourcing through various contractual arrangements for road maintenance works. Under such arrangements, private contractors are responsible for carrying out physical works defined by the government and are paid on the basis of the quantity of civil works executed. Contractors often have a vested interest in executing large, lumpy works, however, and little or no incentive to carry out the many small activities needed to ensure that roads are in good condition over a long period. In addition, governments usually have an incentive to allocate scarce public funds to projects that convey clearly visible benefits to their constituents instead of those that require less visible maintenance expenditures, which often are the first budget items to be cut.

This contracting approach and the general tendency of governments to neglect maintenance have generated a vicious circle of heavy rehabilitation works followed by long periods of neglect and, thus, rapid deterioration. The *World Bank Development Report 1994* estimated that timely maintenance expenditures of US$12 billion would have saved road reconstruction costs of US$45 billion over 10 years (World Bank 1994).

Limited institutional capacity to consistently plan and supervise effective road maintenance has added to the problem.

In an attempt to counteract these limitations, road agencies have begun to adopt performance-based contracting for rehabilitation and maintenance. Performance-based contracts expressly link contractor payments to clearly defined performance standards.[1] Using performance-based contracts offers several potential advantages to road agencies over more traditional approaches, including (a) achieving better road conditions with limited funding available through incentives to the private sector for innovation and higher productivity, and (b) gaining greater certainty about road expenditures to allow for better sectorwide planning. Many of these performance-based contracts would be classified as output-based aid (OBA) approaches, and these approaches are becoming mainstreamed in the roads sector through various types of performance-based maintenance and rehabilitation contracts. For example, in 2003 the World Bank formally adopted (and in 2006 improved) a "Sample Bidding Document for Procurement of Works and Services under Output and Performance-Based Road Contracts," which can be found on the Bank's procurement Web site.

Under OBA schemes in the roads sector, private contractors enter into agreements of a longer nature than traditional road contracts, and the outputs on which they are paid (for example, monthly) relate to the quality of road service provided based on clearly identifiable and measurable parameters (such as average speed obtainable). Thus, the nature of OBA in road maintenance and rehabilitation is quite different from that in other infrastructure sectors in a variety of ways: the ongoing nature of service delivery and the related ongoing subsidy requirement; disbursement of the subsidy (or payment to the service provider) based on a continuing service—management and maintenance of roads—rather than investments; and the public good aspect of roads, whereby no user fee exists and the entire cost to the user is subsidized through public funding, as discussed later in this chapter.[2]

Figure 4.1 shows the widespread use of performance-based contracts in the roads sector. First appearing in Canada in the late 1980s, this approach is now used in many countries and others are considering it, particularly in Asia.

This review has identified 23 projects that involve OBA road contracts within the World Bank Group (figure 4.2), for a total value of US$2.0 billion (excluding more than US$1.7 billion in government subsidy cofinancing), and 11 projects outside the Bank (with the majority in

Figure 4.1   Global Application of Performance-Based Contracting for Roads

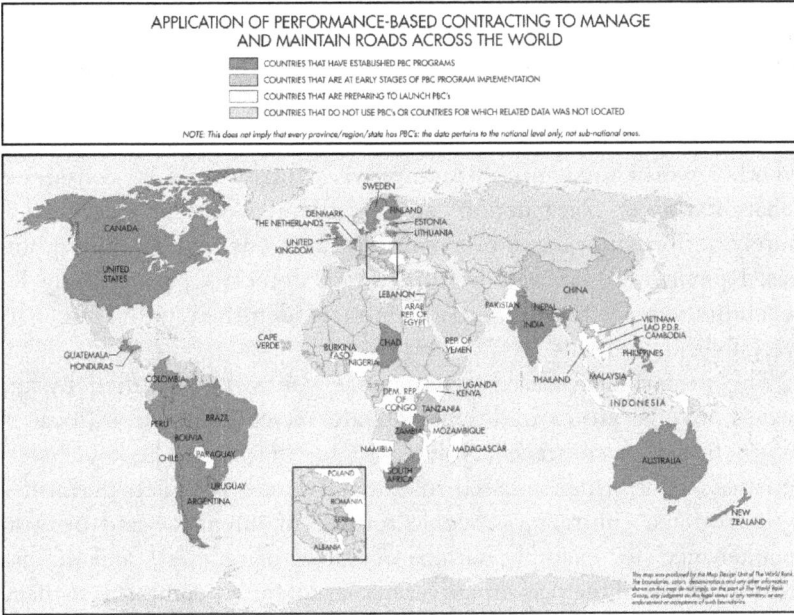

APPLICATION OF PERFORMANCE-BASED CONTRACTING TO MANAGE
AND MAINTAIN ROADS ACROSS THE WORLD

COUNTRIES THAT HAVE ESTABLISHED PBC PROGRAMS
COUNTRIES THAT ARE AT EARLY STAGES OF PBC PROGRAM IMPLEMENTATION
COUNTRIES THAT ARE PREPARING TO LAUNCH PBC's
COUNTRIES THAT DO NOT USE PBC's OR COUNTRIES FOR WHICH RELATED DATA WAS NOT LOCATED

NOTE: This does not imply that every province/region/state has PBC's: the data pertains to the national level only, not sub-national ones.

Source: World Bank 2008d.
Note: PBC = performance-based contract.

**Figure 4.2   Regional Distribution of World Bank Group OBA Projects in Road
Transport**

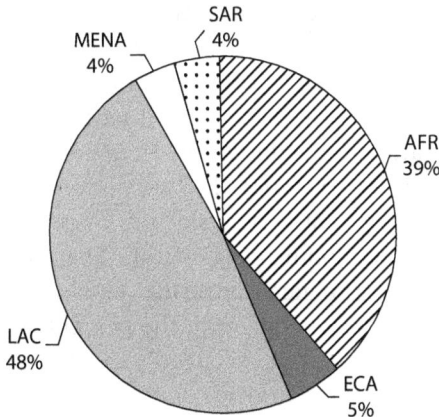

Source: GPOBA database.
Note: Total number of projects is 23. AFR = Africa Region; ECA = Europe and Central Asia Region; LAC = Latin
America and Caribbean Region; MENA = Middle East and North Africa Region; SAR = South Asia Region.

Latin America). These projects fall into two archetypes: (a) performance-based contracts for road maintenance, in which roads are maintained to a specified level of service; and (b) performance-based contracts for rehabilitation and maintenance, in which roads are rehabilitated and then maintained to a specified level of service.

Gray areas exist between the archetypes. For instance, identifying whether works to significantly improve a road should be considered rehabilitation or construction can be difficult. Whether a contract is purely performance based or a hybrid (that is, one that contains input-based payments) can also be difficult to determine, particularly for rehabilitation. Of the OBA road contracts identified, only a minority were hybrid contracts.

The performance-based maintenance contracts identified by the review involve either traditional private sector contractors (local or international) or contracts involving microenterprises. The key characteristics of performance-based road maintenance contracts performed by traditional contractors involve routine maintenance and periodic maintenance (for example, surface treatment or renewal), and the primary objective of the performance-based maintenance contract is to maintain the road asset according to predefined performance standards (Zietlow 2004). In contrast, contracts that engage microenterprises usually cover routine maintenance only and do not involve bidding. Box 4.1 discusses a successful example of a traditional performance-based maintenance contract.

Performance-based rehabilitation and maintenance contracts are based on the performance-based maintenance contract model, but with an added component for rehabilitation: these contracts typically mean bringing a road back to its original serviceable standard. However, an agreed definition of rehabilitation[3] does not appear to exist. The Contrato de Recuperación y Mantenimiento (CREMA) projects in Argentina were among the first performance-based rehabilitation and maintenance contracts outside the Organisation for Economic Co-operation and Development (OECD). The first two phases of Argentina's CREMA program, covering nearly 14,000 kilometers, resulted in significant improvement in the percentage of roads in good condition—from 70 percent in 1998 to 85 percent in 2005. Furthermore, the percentage of roads in poor condition decreased from 8 percent in 1998 to 4.2 percent in 2005 (World Bank 2006b: 4). Many other countries in Latin America have based their performance-based contracts on the CREMA model. Although generally successful,

Box 4.1

Argentina: Pilot Roads Maintenance and Sector Rehabilitation Project

Argentina was the first country not a member of the Organisation for Economic Co-operation and Development to pilot and implement performance-based contracting in the roads sector. A nationwide road survey estimated traffic, defined the minimum (rather than optimum) road standards, defined the rehabilitation and maintenance required, and identified the size and shape of the subnetworks for contracting out work. On the basis of the survey information, the government set uniform, national output indicators for the contracts.

In 1995, 11 contracts were awarded, covering a network of about 3,845 kilometers of paved roads in good to fair condition. Contracts were awarded to the lowest lump-sum bidder. Contractors were paid in equal monthly installments based on the kilometers of road maintained ("kilometer per month" contracts). If the contractor's output did not comply with standards (based on deficiencies noted during monthly inspections), daily penalties were imposed (and subtracted from future payments) until the necessary repairs were carried out.

Inspections were normally carried out on a sample basis, with the minimum length to be inspected weekly representing 5 percent of the total length of the contracted network (or 10 percent if the inspection was for the purpose of establishing payment certificates). The contractor was also required to carry out self-inspections on a daily basis and to report any abnormality—such as traffic overloading—that may have affected the contract or the processes by which the maintenance works were carried out.

Source: Liautaud 2001.

the evolution of the CREMA contracts highlights the fine-tuning necessary to ensure the contract design gives contractors the right incentives to perform, and it demonstrates the balance between the shifting of performance risk to providers and their ability to access finance (see box 9.2 for more details).

Performance-based rehabilitation and maintenance contracts are generally used for roads that are in at least fair condition. As was learned in the Chad roads case (see box 4.2), roads in extremely bad condition are generally not suitable for performance-based contracts for rehabilitation and maintenance because of greater uncertainty for

Box 4.2

Successful Performance-Based Rehabilitation and Maintenance Contracts in Chad

Given the poor results with traditional road maintenance contracts, Chad's government decided to pilot a performance-based contract for the maintenance and management of roads—the National Transport Program Support Project. In late 2000, the government launched a competitive international tender for a contract covering 441 kilometers of continuous, unpaved main roads (7 percent of the primary network). After prequalification, three bidders each presented an offer. In early 2001, the government awarded a four-year performance-based maintenance and management of roads contract to DTP, a subsidiary of the French firm Bouygues.

The bids were evaluated on the basis of the monthly lump-sum fee required. The winning bid came in about 7 percent lower than had been predicted. As long as DTP complied with service quality levels, or outputs, such as average speed attainable, user comfort (often measured by an International Roughness Index), and durability, it will receive a monthly fee of US$480 per kilometer of road serviced. This fee includes fully rehabilitating the road at the outset, managing and maintaining the road for four years, monitoring compliance with the performance criteria, and providing basic aid in road accidents, among others. DTP received an advance payment of 20 percent of the contract value, for which it had to provide a guarantee. It also had to provide a performance guarantee of 10 percent of the contract value.

DTP had 22 months to raise service quality to the required levels. It complied with and, in many cases, exceeded the requirements for service quality levels. With the roads in good condition, only ongoing maintenance was required. Chad's government split the 441 kilometers of road into two sections and bid out both sections under performance-based contracts. Different local contractors won, and still hold, these contracts. Performance-based contracting has now been extended to Chad's rural roads. Eight local contractors have partially rehabilitated and now maintain Chad's most important rural roads through the dry season.

Sources: Hartwig, Mumssen, and Schliessler 2005; author discussion with Andreas Schliessler, Senior Transport Specialist, World Bank, October 2008.

both government and contractors about the nature and extent of work required to bring these roads to a maintainable standard. In addition, the greater the proportion of rehabilitation costs to maintenance costs, the greater the contractor's incentive to renege on the contract after rehabilitation is completed.

Funding

For most of the roads projects identified, contributions from international donors form a significant component of overall funding. These donors largely include the IDA, the IBRD, and bilateral aid agencies (for example, the U.S. Agency for International Development). Other funding sources include other international agencies, such as the United Nations Development Programme and the United Nations Economic Commission for Latin America and the Caribbean.

Governments also contribute funding, increasingly through dedicated road maintenance funds provided by, for example, fuel taxes. Road maintenance funds can impart further stability to a government's portion of the contract by ensuring a sustainable source of funding for road maintenance that is independent of the government's other fiscal constraints and obligations.[4] Dedicated road funds are more widely used in OECD countries; the review found limited evidence of road funds being used in OBA schemes in developing countries. For example, even Argentina and Brazil do not use road funds to support their OBA schemes.

Through the 1970s, governments tended to earmark general tax revenues for road maintenance. This allocation depended on the annual political budget, so these conventional, or first-generation, road funds were often unsuccessful in securing stable and reliable funding. The International Monetary Fund and many finance ministries also opposed this approach because it earmarked revenues unrelated to road use and did not always provide the flexibility required if governments needed to allocate funding for new priorities. Therefore, this "tension" between the sustainability of the funding source required for a viable road fund and the flexibility required for governments to reallocate budgets when necessary needed to be balanced. Many countries have since established second-generation road funds (ADB 2003). These funds operate under a user-pay model, collecting fees through a two-part tariff consisting primarily of an access fee (vehicle license fees and a supplementary heavy vehicle fee) and a user fee (a fuel levy, international transit fees, and fines for overloading). To help provide more efficient use of resources, second-generation road funds are sometimes created at arm's length from government, with a public-private board managing the fund.

By providing long-term sustainable funding of road maintenance, road maintenance funds can increase a government's ability to pursue performance-based road maintenance contracts. Unlike performance-based contracts for capital works, performance-based road maintenance contracts require governments to make payments to contractors on a regular basis. Road maintenance funds reassure contractors that governments will meet contractual commitments to pay by creating a sustainable source of funding that is independent of the government's other fiscal constraints and obligations.

Targeting

The public good characteristics of roads make it difficult to target road subsidies to a specific group of beneficiaries. As long as road use is unrivaled (that is, not congested), excluding users would decrease economic welfare. Where road use is rivaled (that is, congested), an OBA scheme could consist of a toll road, where the copayment (toll) varies by income. No examples were found in developing countries in the sample reviewed.

The fact that OBA road projects do not tend to specifically target the poor does not suggest that the poor do not benefit significantly from these projects. In the Chad projects, for example, the national road network was selected for upgrading because it benefited poor rural communities more than upgrading the local roads used by these communities (Hartwig, Mumssen, and Schliessler 2005).

Performance Risk

Under OBA road contracts, the road agency specifies performance standards that the contractor is required to meet when delivering maintenance services. Payments generally depend on whether the contractor complies with the performance standards and not on the amount of work and services executed. For example, the contractor is paid not for the number of patched potholes but for the output of his work: having no pothole remain open or unpatched. Failure to comply with the performance indicators or to promptly rectify deficiencies adversely affects the contractor's payment through a series of clearly defined penalties. The choice and application of technology and the pursuit of innovative materials, processes, and management are up to the contractor rather than specified by the agency.

When the agency upholds these criteria, the contractor bears much of the risk for its failure of management and innovation. Such failures can include errors in predicting deterioration of contracted assets; determining appropriate design, specifications, and materials; and planning needed maintenance interventions (Stankevich, Qureshi, and Queiroz 2005). The contractor also has opportunities to increase margins where improved efficiencies and effectiveness of design, process, technology, or management are able to reduce the cost of achieving the specified performance standards.

Overall, performance-based road contracts have shifted more ongoing service delivery risk to contractors compared to traditional forced accounts or contracting. Such contracts have, for example, reduced the share of roads in poor condition in Argentina from 25 percent to 5 percent and increased the average road maintenance rating from 51 percent to 87 percent, well above the agreed minimum standard defined in the performance contract, while at the same time allowing the government funding agency to save money (National Highway Maintenance Contract Seminar 2005; Segal, Moore, and McCarthy 2003).

Performance-based contracts for maintenance typically specify performance standards, or service quality outputs, that a contractor must meet to be paid. The contractor's performance is then measured against these outputs. Performance standards vary from contract to contract and from country to country (table 4.1).

Table 4.1   Performance Indicators for Transport Projects

Contracts	Performance indicators
CREMA (for example, Argentina, Brazil)	Potholes; cracking and rutting; condition of shoulders, culverts, and drains; roadside environment; guardrails; vertical and horizontal signs
Cape Verde, Chad, Madagascar, Tanzania	Passability (open road), average speed attainable, user comfort (often measured by an International Roughness Index), durability (a measure of the long-term sustainability of the road)
South Africa's Routine Road Maintenance Project	Clean and visible road signs, grass cutting

Source: GPOBA database.

Road contracts have linked payment to performance in a variety of methods:

- *Advance payment.* For example, in Argentina, this payment was 20 percent.
- *Fixed monthly payment.* In Argentina, the contractor is paid in terms of dollars per month per kilometer, and microenterprise contractors receive a fixed monthly fee in equal installments.
- *Penalties for noncompliance.* Penalties for noncompliance are deducted from monthly payments. For example, some microenterprises receive penalties on a scale of 5 to 10 percent or demerit points.

Generally, contracts performed by microenterprises have fewer—and simpler—performance standards for routine maintenance than those performed by traditional contractors. Very few cooperative microenterprises have been terminated due to noncompliance. Strong incentives to comply tend to prevail because of a microenterprise's need for timely payment, owing to a lack of capital to survive an extended period of nonpayment.

In rehabilitation and maintenance contracts in Argentina and Brazil, the contract specifies the sections of the road that need rehabilitation and the "minimum solution required to ensure a positive net present value for the investment." The contractor is then free to propose any rehabilitation solution above the "minimum solution" (Liautaud 2001: 2). The rehabilitation solution proposed by the contractor is then used as the contracted output standard. Performance indicators for rehabilitation normally include that rehabilitation works must (a) meet or exceed the minimum thickness of overlay, and (b) not exceed the maximum level of roughness, rut depth, cracking, or raveling (Liautaud 2001).

The Chad pilot took a different approach. Rather than requiring rehabilitation of the full length of the road before maintenance began, and setting separate performance standards for that period, the government of Chad simply set performance standards and a timetable for the contractor to reach those standards. The contractor's obligations to bring the road up to standard increased gradually (for example, by month 12, 50 percent of the roads had to meet the set standard). A similar approach was taken in the pilots in Cape Verde, Madagascar, and Tanzania and in the subsequent performance-based contracts in Chad.

Private Sector Capital and Expertise

For the performance-based projects reviewed, services were contracted to private firms. The types of private firm varied by project, including the following:

- Local firm (for example, Argentina pilot)
- International firm (for example, Chad pilot)
- Single-owner microenterprise (for example, Guatemala, Peru)
- Cooperative microenterprises (for example, Bolivia, Colombia, Ecuador, Honduras, Nicaragua, República Bolivariana de Venezuela, South Africa)

Many of the maintenance contracts reviewed were contracted to microenterprises. Microenterprises need considerable training and support; a microenterprise needs about one year to become functional. In addition, when local contractors are involved, a partnership approach often exists between the World Bank, the roads department, and local contractors, because the government and local contractors need to acquire skills and adjust to this new approach.

Another innovative approach that exhibits OBA characteristics is the annuity road contract arrangement being implemented throughout India. The India Roads Annuity Project involves a performance-based contract to build and maintain a road (see box 4.3).

Box 4.3

Annuity Concessions in India

Transport sector spending in India has been declining steadily over the years, and a severe shortage exists of public funds for road construction and maintenance. To address this problem, the government has introduced private sector participation by allowing private operators to collect tolls on public and private roads. The National Highways Authority of India (NHAI) developed the annuity concession model for roads where revenue from tolls is uncertain or insufficient to attract build-operate-transfer operators. Approximately 8 percent of the length of roadways subject to funding by the NHAI has been commissioned using the annuity concession model.

(continued)

Box 4.3 *(Continued)*

In annuity concessions, the private operator is remunerated through a fixed, periodic annuity payment from NHAI and is responsible for constructing the road and also operating and maintaining the road for a fixed period. The government determines the annuity payment based on the total cost of the project, likely annual maintenance expenses, contract period, and prevailing interest rate, among other criteria. This payment begins only when construction has been completed to specified quality standards.

The annuity concession model rewards early completion and provides the private operator with a built-in incentive to ensure that the road is constructed to minimize long-term operation and maintenance costs while meeting quality standards. The focus on performance has reduced the cost of government monitoring required during the construction period and has resulted in construction costs that are on average 12 to 35 percent lower than NHAI's estimates. The annuity concession model is now a widely employed form of public-private partnership in India and has been particularly successful at attracting domestic private investors. As of April 2007, 24 projects (totaling 1,340 kilometers) have been implemented on an annuity basis.

Sources: Booth 2006; National Portal of India, "Public-Private Partnership," http://india.gov.in/sectors/transport/public_private.php.

Monitoring

The outputs, or indicators, monitored in road projects include conditions of the road and road shoulder (for example, the number of potholes for a given distance of road monitored); passability and average speed attainable on the road; and visibility of road signs. The indicators together provide a picture of the usability of the road and thus demonstrate the degree of improved access provided for intended users.

Monitoring and evaluation of performance-based road contracts are conducted through a range of methods: self-monitoring, government, and independent consultant (used especially when a road agency is short staffed or might need extra support for innovative contracting mechanisms). Often, projects use a combination of these methods, as in the following examples:

- *CREMA.* Government engineers conduct monthly on-site inspections, normally carried out on a sample basis, with the minimum road length to be inspected weekly representing 5 percent of the total length of the contracted network (or 10 percent if the inspection is to establish payment certificates). The minimum elementary length of inspection is 2 kilometers. The contractor is also required to make its own inspection on a daily basis and to report to the engineer any abnormality (such as traffic overloading) that may affect the contract or the processes used to carry out the maintenance works. Likewise, accidents attributable to users are to be reported, especially when they involve damages to the infrastructure itself.

- *Chad.* First, the contractor performs self-monitoring, submitting a report to the government with each monthly invoice. Second, a consultant verifies the self-monitoring reports through monthly inspections. (The government appointed SADEG, an engineering consulting firm in Cameroon, for this monitoring role.) If the contractor fails to comply with any of the service criteria in any one month, its fee is reduced. If it fails repeatedly to comply, its contract can be suspended.

Monitoring and evaluation can also involve road users. For example, in some CREMA contracts, representatives of the user community periodically are allowed to participate in inspections.

Notes

1. A performance-based contract is also known as a performance-based management and maintenance contract, output-based service contract, and performance-specified maintenance contract. These names are often used interchangeably. The term *OBA* is rarely used for these contracts other than for output and performance-based road contracts; *performance-based* alone is used more commonly.

2. All OBA schemes in developing countries indentified in the transport sector were in the roads subsector. A few transport services schemes were considered but are not far along enough in design or implementation to be included in this review.

3. *Rehabilitation* of paved roads is defined as selective repair and strengthening of the pavement or shoulder after partial demolition of the existing structure (Zeitlow 2004).

4. Although the CREMA contracts did not involve a road fund, the long-term payment obligations were made legally binding on the government of Argentina and helped deter the treasury from reneging on road maintenance funding at times of fiscal constraint (for example, in 1998-99 and at the end of 2001). The budget process respected that CREMA contracts and funds were a priority and considered them nondiscretionary expenditures (http://www.worldbank.org/transport/roads/resource-guide/Case-Argentina.htm).

## CHAPTER 5

Energy

Traditionally, expansion of energy access in many developing countries has involved public utilities preparing technical feasibility studies for conventional grid extension and then procuring equipment and works. Customers must pay high connection fees and internal installation costs. This approach has often failed because of public utilities' lack of financial capacity, inefficiency of providers that leads to increased costs, and customers' limited ability to pay.

Output-based aid (OBA) is one approach being implemented in the energy sector to improve access and targeting for the poor. In the World Bank Group (WBG), 30 OBA schemes in the energy sector have been identified. Figure 5.1 demonstrates the regional breakdown of WBG OBA energy projects by number of projects and by total value of OBA subsidy.

Several additional schemes have been identified outside the World Bank, among them a number of projects funded by the Netherlands Directorate-General for International Cooperation through the Energizing Africa Initiative. This initiative has provided funding for 24 projects expected to provide energy, mostly through off-grid solutions, to over 5 million poor beneficiaries in Africa.

Although OBA made a later start in the energy sector than in the information and communication technology and roads sectors, the sector

Figure 5.1   Regional Distribution of World Bank Group OBA Energy Projects

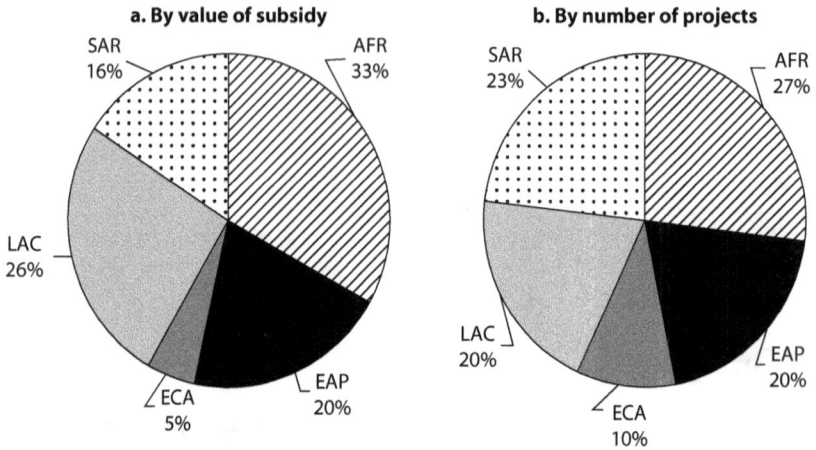

a. By value of subsidy

b. By number of projects

Source: GPOBA database.
Note: Total subsidy in panel a = US$204 million. Total projects in panel b = 30. AFR = Sub-Saharan Africa Region; EAP = East Asia and Pacific Region; ECA = Europe and Central Asia Region; LAC = Latin America and Caribbean Region; SAR = South Asia Region.

has gained much ground. OBA has been most prevalent in rural energy. In fact, OBA is becoming one of the main tools used for expanding off-grid access, where outputs are often defined as the installation of a functioning off-grid unit, such as solar home systems (SHSs). OBA is also being used in grid and minigrid schemes, in which outputs are usually defined as working connections to the network. However, as a proportion of total grid and minigrid schemes, OBA has yet to make as strong a mark. Nevertheless, the creation and expansion of rural energy funds to increase access in rural areas may be a platform from which to scale up and mainstream OBA in the energy sector.

OBA might be more prevalent in rural electrification schemes for some of the following reasons:

- Rural electrification rates are lower than urban electrification rates. Hence, a greater relative need for expanded access exists in rural areas.
- Costs of expansion are greater in rural areas, and the need for subsidies is greater than in urban areas where providers have relatively greater incentives for expansion.
- Rural energy schemes allow for new entrants and greater competition and, hence, potential private sector participation.

- Many urban infrastructure access schemes can become complicated by the issue of illegal settlements, land titles, and other related issues that are politically sensitive and, therefore, may lead to reluctance to target these areas with subsidies.
- The characteristics of rural off-grid technologies are well suited for one-off subsidy design, because individual systems with high upfront costs and relatively low requirements for operations and maintenance provide the service.

The review of OBA in energy is segmented into off-grid, minigrid, and grid-based systems.

Off-Grid Systems

The use of output-based subsidies in the energy sector is most widespread in individual systems for rural electrification. The predominant technology used for individual systems in off-grid projects is photovoltaic (PV), mainly SHS (Terrado, Cabraal, and Mukherjee 2008). More than 15 SHS OBA projects have been identified. Other available technologies to power individual systems include wind, pico-hydro, and biogas, among others. The outputs on which subsidies are disbursed usually include the installation of a functioning off-grid unit—the SHS.

Two main business models—the dealer and the fee-for-service models—are currently being used to deliver or distribute SHSs in rural areas, and OBA has been used in most of these cases to increase affordability and thereby improve access. The choice of a business model depends on existing government policy and regulatory capacity, availability of potential suppliers or service providers, user affordability, and the availability of credit or access to finance, among other criteria.

Dealer model. Under this model, consumers own the stand-alone systems, and private dealers sell systems on a cash or credit basis in the open market.[1] The customer is responsible for maintenance following the warranty period provided by the dealer or manufacturer. Dealers can be private companies or nongovernmental organizations (NGOs). The dealer model usually requires the accreditation of several participating dealers and establishment of a microfinance support system, as needed (Terrado, Cabraal, and Mukherjee 2008). Some dealers themselves extend credit to purchasers of PV systems (dealer-credit model). In either case, the OBA subsidy is generally used to buy down the capital cost and is paid after installation is verified (see box 5.1 on Bangladesh's Rural Electrification and Renewable Energy Development [RERED] Project).

Box 5.1

Bangladesh: Rural Electrification and Renewable Energy Development Project (2002–09)

Bangladesh's Rural Electrification and Renewable Energy Development Project was launched in 2002 with the objective to increase access to electricity in rural areas. The SHS component, financed by a Global Environment Facility (GEF) grant of US$8.2 million for capital cost buy-down, was implemented as an OBA. Private companies in partnership with microfinance institutions (MFIs) and NGOs supply and service the SHSs. The Infrastructure Development Company Limited (IDCOL), the service provider, administers a credit program that enables participating NGOs and MFIs to obtain refinancing for loans made to households for the purchase of SHSs.

The GEF grants are contingent on actual installation of systems. The grants are drawn and disbursed by IDCOL against claims made by MFIs and suppliers on prescribed documentation and evidence that solar systems have been installed and accepted. The cost of the SHS (on average, US$500) is met by a GEF grant of about US$40–50 per system, a customer's down payment, and a microfinance loan covering the balance.

The project successfully installed its target of 50,000 SHSs by September 2005, three years ahead of schedule and US$2 million below the estimated project cost. Following such success, IDCOL has received funding from KfW (Kreditanstalt für Wiederaufbau), GTZ (German Agency for Technical Cooperation), the Asian Development Bank, and the Islamic Development Bank to fund a total of approximately 500,000 SHSs. As of July 2009, more than 334,000 SHSs had been installed. In August 2009, the World Bank approved a US$130 million credit to finance an additional 300,000 SHSs and extend credit for the development of renewable energy minigrids in rural Bangladesh. This may be enhanced with several million in co-funding from GPOBA and SIDA to reach many more poor rural households.

Sources: IDCOL Web site, http://www.idcol.org; GPOBA Commitment Paper: OBA for Rural Electrification and Renewable Energy Development in Bangladesh, August 2009, p. 9, section A.1.

Fee-for-service model. Under this model, public or private organizations retain ownership of the systems and provide electricity services for a fee. The leasing or hire-purchase model and the Energy Service Company (ESCO) model are both fee-for-service models. Under a concession model, an ESCO is usually selected by a competitive process and given the exclusive right to provide electricity services in a defined service area. The OBA subsidy is generally used to buy down the capital cost and make the monthly payment in line with the users' ability to pay (see box 5.2).

In the dealer model, OBA subsidies are one-off, whereas in the fee-for-service model, the OBA subsidy can have both a one-off component and an ongoing component.

A third model that is emerging is a hybrid between the dealer model and the fee-for-service model known as the medium-term service contract (MSC). The MSC is a new model for PV market development that balances the providers' wish to minimize risk exposure with the government's desire to maximize control. In all service areas, exclusive access to project subsidies ends three to four years after installation, at which time users and suppliers may graduate to open competition. The MSC design for the contracts between government and service provider goes well beyond the typical connection (and sometimes service) targets of comparable energy projects, by disbursing a portion of subsidies against activities promoting market development on the local microlevel in each area to ensure long-term sustainability of service and market growth. Bolivia's Decentralized Infrastructure for Rural Transformation (Infraestructura

---

Box 5.2

The ESCO Model: Argentina PERMER Concession

The ESCO model demonstrates how OBA can mobilize private sector expertise to provide services to poor households that might not otherwise be reached. In Argentina's Renewable Energies in the Rural Market Project (Proyecto de Energía Renovable en el Mercado Eléctrico Rural; PERMER), concessions were awarded competitively for a period of 15 years. Concessionaires were required to provide electricity services to rural off-grid customers anywhere in the province for a period of 15 years, upon request. Customers who could not be reached by the grid were served with SHSs, whose installation was subsidized by GEF grants. The concessionaire is responsible for all necessary maintenance, repairs, or replacement of components. It is also responsible for billing, collection, and claims handling. The provincial government and provincial utility regulatory agency review or renegotiate the fees and tariffs every two years. As of November 2008, Argentina's PERMER had provided 8,000 households and 1,900 schools with access to electricity, primarily through solar and wind technology systems.

Sources: Reiche, Covarrubias, and Martinot 2000; World Bank 2008a, 2008c.

Descentralizada para la Transformación Rural; IDTR), funded by the International Development Association (IDA), is an example of such a scheme.

Minigrid Systems

The use of OBA schemes for expanding rural electrification through minigrids has been limited; about five projects have been identified. Minigrids involve a centrally located generating system that serves tens or hundreds of users. A minigrid is an attractive option when customers are concentrated enough to be economically interconnected but cannot be feasibly connected to the main grid. Most of the projects identified involve minihydro or minidiesel systems. The outputs on which subsidies are disbursed in minigrid systems are diverse and can range from construction milestones to installed capacity to connection of new customers. Most projects identified include a mix of these outputs, but most rely on one-off subsidies for access. In terms of market model, public-private partnerships in the form of concession contracts are the most common. Under concessions, the service provider has exclusive rights to generate, distribute, and sell electricity in the concession area.

Grid-Based Systems

OBA is being used in several instances to expand access to the urban and peri-urban poor through grid-based extensions. For example, the Armenia Heating and Gas project provides heating solutions to eligible households in apartment buildings. The project funds both individual gas-heater solutions for apartments and building-level gas-boiler solutions that connect several apartments. As of July 2009, over 60 percent (2,825) of the target households had received heating solutions that had been independently verified. A grant agreement for a slum electrification scheme in Mumbai has recently been signed. In this scheme, GPOBA will pay a portion of the slum dwellers' costs to licensed contractors for installing internal wiring and new or upgraded electricity connections from the meter to the house using an OBA approach. Reliance Energy (the privately owned local distribution company) will carry out upstream investment to improve supply to the slum as part of the project.

Similarly, the outputs on which subsidies are typically disbursed in rural grid-based schemes are verified working connections. More specialized output indicators are added wherever possible to reflect the project's main objectives. For example, Ethiopia's Electricity Access Rural Expansion Project II, funded by GPOBA and IDA, is both accelerating the pace of connections in electrified areas and fostering energy efficiency by including two compact fluorescent lamps as part of the connection package to poor households.

In addition to one-off subsidies, transitional and ongoing output-based subsidies have been used in grid-based schemes. The Pamir Private Power Project in Tajikistan uses a combination of transitional and ongoing consumption subsidies to ensure that tariffs remain affordable for the residents of the Gorno-Badakshan region. The Pamir social protection scheme uses a very low lifeline block tariff aimed at ensuring that the poorest can afford a minimal (lifeline) amount of electricity; for consumption over the lifeline amount, the tariff gradually rises to full cost levels. In contrast, the Philippines Non-Grid Power Supply project, a small power utility group (SPUG), uses ongoing output-based subsidies to improve electricity supply in remote areas. The ongoing subsidies (US$0.028 per kilowatt-hour for the first pilot) are paid on the basis of the energy supplied to the rural energy distribution cooperatives (not on the basis of the electricity produced) by the competitively selected private generators. The first SPUG transaction, expected to be fully operational by the end of 2009, will improve electricity service for nearly 60,000 households and result in US$7 million subsidy savings in the first year of operation.

Funding

The major sources of funding for output-based energy projects are international and bilateral donors, government cofinancing, user contributions, and private sector investment. The level of funding from each of these sources depends on project-specific factors, which include location of the project, type of technology used, users' ability to pay, and local credit markets, among others.

Minigrid projects are highly capital intensive and are typically funded by the government or donors or both. Grid-based projects vary: grid intensification in urban areas is less capital intensive than grid extension in peri-urban or rural areas. In Ethiopia's Electricity Access Rural Expansion Project II, 90 percent of the total project cost of US$203 million was funded by various donors, including IDA (US$130.0 million in credit) and the Ethiopian government through the public utility Ethiopian Electric Power Corporation (US$44.4 million). The remaining 10 percent is expected to come from user payments.

In off-grid projects, donors such as Global Environment Facility (GEF), IDA, and KfW provided initial funding for subsidizing these technologies to make them more competitive and commercially viable. GEF also provided funding for the critical business and market development activities, such as feasibility studies, consumer awareness, credit delivery, and so forth. Private sector financing is also leveraged (see discussion below).

Many projects such as Guatemala's Rural Electrification Plan (Plan de Electrificación Rural; PER) and Senegal's Rural Electrification Priority Program (PPER) have dedicated Rural Electrification Funds (REFs) to ensure rural electrification goals are met without competing with other social and infrastructure needs. In Guatemala's PER, the rural electrification fund raised US$100 million through the sale of the distribution companies to private operators and US$50 million from the sale of government bonds (Harris 2002; 2). Additional funding of US$180 million was being sought from other donors. In this specific case, the WBG contribution was in the form of a US$96.6 million guarantee by the Multilateral Investment Guarantee Agency, extended to Unión Fenosa Internacional, S.A., providing insurance coverage for the privatization of two state-run power distribution companies, also part of Guatemala's PER (see Guatemala's Rural Electrification Plan in the appendix). These REFs are also financed through other sources, such as a surcharge on all existing users (for example, the Philippines SPUG project).

Targeting

Most OBA energy projects use a blend of geographic targeting (selecting poorer locations where subsidies should be channeled) and self-selection targeting (subsidizing outputs that the nonpoor are less likely to use).

Initially, off-grid projects primarily used geographic targeting. However, the traditional approach to subsidy was sometimes regressive because it typically used constant relative subsidies (dollar per watt-peak), which penalized the poor, who ultimately paid relatively higher lifecycle costs because of size-independent fixed costs (Reiche, Rysankova, and Goldmark 2006: 31). Later projects have addressed this issue by using self-selection targeting. For example, in Bolivia's IDTR, because the absolute subsidy per system is constant, the subsidy per watt-peak increases the smaller the system, and the poor are more likely to use smaller systems. As of February 2009, 6,154 individual systems had been installed under IDTR, benefiting more than 30,000 people in remote rural areas of Bolivia. In addition, 87 social systems had been installed in schools and clinics. The poorest households that are unable to afford the subsidized SHS can benefit from the electrification of rural schools and health clinics as well as the multiplier effects expected from rural productive uses. In addition, the GPOBA replication of IDTR plans to introduce low-end pico-PV solutions specifically targeted to the poorest. These systems will provide basic lighting and information and communication technology, as well as dry cell charging for less than US$100 per household.

The grid-based rural electrification project in Guatemala involves two distribution companies that were sold to a private operator; the proceeds of the sale were used to fund an OBA scheme based on geographic targeting. Households that live more than 200 meters from the existing network receive the connection subsidy based on the assumption that those households are more likely to be poor. Although not without problems, the coverage results have been good (over 80 percent of the initially targeted population has been connected).

Two grid-based natural gas OBA schemes in middle-income countries target OBA subsidies to households already classified as poor through broader welfare or related programs. One of the outputs in an IDA-GPOBA urban gas project in Armenia is defined as a solution based on individual gas heaters for households living on an average per capita income of approximately US$0.50 per day. By verifying that beneficiaries of the OBA subsidy are actually registered in the official social protection program supporting low-income households in Armenia, the output verification ensures that the subsidy is targeted and actually delivered to eligible households. One of the primary output criteria in Colombia's project for Natural Gas Distribution for Low-Income Families in the Caribbean Coast is proof that each newly connected household belongs to one of Colombia's two poorest economic strata as officially classified with an average per capita income of less than US$1 per day. To avoid excluding the poorest from benefiting from the service, the project also includes the provision of a basic gas stove.

A delayed phase-in of subsidies can be used as a form of self-selection targeting, because households that can afford an unsubsidized connection fee will connect to a service when the service is initially available if the benefits of connecting outweigh the cost. This mechanism is being piloted in an energy project funded by GPOBA and IDA in Ethiopia that subsidizes grid connection in rural areas.

In addition to the connection costs, the costs of internal wiring can be a significant hurdle and could lead to low uptake. For a solution to this affordability barrier, projects such as Senegal's PPER include a payment facility for spreading out the capital costs of connection, internal wiring, and efficient fluorescent lamps—making these far more affordable for even the poorest households. How this facility will work is yet to be seen because the project has not yet begun to deliver outputs.

Performance Risk

The degree of performance risk that is shifted to the service provider largely depends on the ability of potential service providers to bear such risk and access short-term financing prior to the disbursement of output-based subsidies.

Outputs in off-grid energy projects are mainly defined as the installation of the off-grid technology to provide electrification (for example, SHS, biogas digesters, and so forth). The most common practice has been to pay the entire subsidy on successful verification of eligible installation irrespective of the service delivery model. Not many instances occur in which subsidy disbursements are linked to service delivery and maintenance. Current exceptions include Bolivia's IDTR and Ghana's SHS projects recently under implementation:

- In Bolivia, 3 percent of the subsidies is paid after each of the three yearly service visits, and the final 5 percent is paid at the end of the contract agreement (three-year MSC) and upon completion of all obligations. The service contracts were originally set at four years, but after the prebidding road shows, the market clearly indicated that a four-year contract would attract fewer bidders.
- In Ghana, 80 percent of the subsidies is paid after installation, 5 percent against completion of maintenance services at the end of each of years 1 and 2, and the 10 percent final payment against one battery replacement and satisfactory maintenance services at the end of year 3.

Lessons from early experience suggest that credit risk is a serious concern of both financiers and dealers and makes credit sales particularly challenging. Dealers are reluctant to extend credit to rural customers with little credit history, and credit administration and collections may be costly. Dealer-extended credit was tried early in a Sri Lanka project (see the next section of this chapter, "Private Sector Capital and Expertise") but was soon rejected. Dealers found collections too difficult and time consuming (World Bank 2008b: 137). As a result, they formed partner-ships with microfinance organizations for extending consumer credit. Similarly, the IDA line of credit extended to the rural banks in Ghana is expected to help mitigate some of the constraints on access to finance and credit faced by dealers or purchasers, or both.

The performance risks are higher for the ESCO by virtue of the concession model and not only because of the OBA design. The service provider takes on commercial, technical, and investment risk because it gets paid for all the investments over time from the monthly fees paid by users. The service provider collects monthly payments from its customers and provides maintenance service as needed. In some cases, some of this monthly payment relates to the subsidy buy-down of the capital costs. For example, in the South African Concession for Rural Electrification project, the ongoing subsidy for free basic electricity for grid-connected households equivalent to 50 kilowatt-hours per month was introduced to encourage electricity consumption among the grid-connected rural households. In contrast, SHS users in the concession areas received an equivalent monthly subsidy of R 40, reducing the fee charged for maintaining and servicing the system to R 20 (from R 60) per month for each household. However, not all municipalities within a concession honored the ongoing SHS subsidy, creating distortions between consumers (Lemaire 2007: 6).

Outputs in grid-based and minigrid OBA schemes are usually working connections to the network, but they may involve a wider variety of milestones. Up-front capital expenditures as a percentage of total costs are very high for minigrids, and the providers are typically small. Therefore, a larger fraction of the subsidy must be paid up front to avoid increasing the financing costs and hence the subsidy levels. In Nicaragua's Offgrid Rural Electrification Project (Proyecto de Electrificación Rural en Zonas Aisladas; PERZA), up to 70 percent of the output-based subsidies are disbursed early (against installation of turbines and grid) whereas only a smaller fraction of the subsidy (20–30 percent) is disbursed against new connections and service quality (Reiche, Rysankova, and Goldmark 2006: 26). As of December 2008, 2,426 households had been successfully connected to three minigrids under the PERZA project, benefiting more than 12,000 beneficiaries. Additionally, the PERZA project had funded the installation of 6,863 SHSs, reaching more than 34,000 beneficiaries.

The performance risk taken by service providers related to the OBA element of grid-based electrification schemes varies. In some cases, the

OBA performance risk relates to payment of a subsidy after the connection is fully installed and working as verified by an independent agent. When providers have long-term contracts, performance risk also relates to longer-term service provision, although this risk is not necessarily specifically related to the OBA scheme.

In Senegal's PPER project, the average cost of connection is estimated at US$725 and the average subsidy at about US$286. The difference—accounting for 60 percent of the project costs, or a total of US$10 million—is to be entirely borne by the competitively selected private operator, Office National de l'Electricité (ONE) of Morocco. ONE is likely to undertake significant investment and performance risk because these investments will largely be recovered by monthly payments over the concession term of 25 years. Furthermore, the subsidy is to be disbursed in tranches, with the final 40 percent made only after the rural electrification agency has verified the number of customers connected and certified that minimum technical standards as stipulated in the concession have been met. However, this ambitious concession arrangement has not yet delivered the specified outputs (see box 5.3 for more details).

In contrast, the US$26 million investment under the Pamir Private Power Project was made to restore reliable electricity supply to 250,000 poor and isolated residents of Tajikistan's Gorno-Badakshan region. From the start, the project clearly was not feasible on a commercial basis. As mentioned earlier, the project uses a combination of both transitional and ongoing consumption subsidies to ensure that tariffs paid by households remain affordable. The subsidies (the difference between full cost and subsidized tariff) are paid only upon delivery of the electricity service.

Box 5.3

Senegal's Rural Electrification Priority Program

The government of Senegal, with assistance from the World Bank, adopted the Rural Electrification Priority Program in 2003. The PPER combines privately operated concessions with output-based subsidies to leverage private financial resources and overcome the barrier of high up-front connection costs. Under the PPER, the country was divided into 13 concessions (updated from the original 18). Moreover, private utilities traditionally have had little incentive to connect poor households in remote areas because their concession contracts limit their service

(continued)

Box 5.3 *(Continued)*

obligation to households located a relatively short distance from the grid. Senegal's PPER concession explicitly addresses this issue by requiring the concessionaire to make a minimum number of connections beyond 20 kilometers from the grid.

The bidding process for the first concession, Dagana-Podor, was launched successfully in June 2006, with eight firms (local, regional, and international) participating in the prequalification and two final bids: ONE from Morocco and a consortium of EDF, Total, and Senegal's CSI-Matforce. The winning bidder, ONE, has proposed to more than double the minimum number of connections set in the tender—growing from 8,500 to 21,800—by bringing in US$9.6 million in private financing. This share constitutes about 60 percent of the total financing, compared to the 20 percent minimum private financing required under the tender. The average cost for a connection is estimated at US$725 and the average subsidy at about US$286. ONE also has proposed to increase both the overall number of connections and the proportion of connections using renewables, which means the benefits of both the IDA and the GEF subsidies will be maximized. The International Finance Corporation (IFC) is expected to decide on a potential equity investment (up to 19.99 percent) in the project company, Comasel de Saint Louis S.A. If the investment is approved by the IFC board, it would be the IFC's first venture into rural electrification.

The Dagana-Podor concession with ONE was finally officially signed in June 2008. The scheme has many positive design attributes from which to learn, but at the same time, is an ambitious scheme that has yet to deliver on its great promise at the time of this writing.

Sources: de Gouvello and Kumar 2007; International Finance Corporation, http://www.ifc.org/.

Private Sector Capital and Expertise

Dealers for off-grid energy schemes are typically small and medium-size operators that have limited capacity to take credit risk for extending loans to rural households and lack experience in credit-facility management. Yet small-scale private providers are taking risks in OBA schemes. For example, in Sri Lanka's RERED project, three SHS dealers have each made investments estimated at US$1 million to US$1.5 million to develop the systems, physical infrastructure, and human resources for a commercial distribution network of 50 sales and service outlets with motivated sales forces, trained technicians, and good product and brand awareness

(World Bank 2002). Although the amounts are small in absolute terms, the relative risks are substantial from the perspective of the small private dealers. This effort seems to be paying off. By June 2008, some 120,000 households were using SHSs in Sri Lanka (Terrado, Cabraal, and Mukherjee 2008: 5). In Bangladesh's RERED project, sales of SHSs are financed by a customer's initial contribution (about 15 percent), a GEF grant, and the credit purchase loan—of which 80 percent is refinanced by Infrastructure Development Company Limited (IDCOL). Part of the project's success is the result of abetting NGO and multifinance institution operators to operate as SHS vendors. In parallel, technical assistance provided during the start-up phase (approximately January to December 2002) enabled the private operators to quickly gain proficiency in the SHS business. To increase the ability of microfinance institutions to provide loans that will encourage more widespread adoption of SHSs, an IDA line of credit of US$11.4 million was made available for Bangladesh's project to provide long-term credit refinancing to eligible MFIs for financing of households' or individuals' purchases of SHSs. Over time, the private operators have reduced the interest charged to consumers, and already the largest-volume supplier (Grameen Shakti) has reduced the interest to a flat 6 percent (World Bank 2005a).

In the case of ESCOs, obtaining commercial loans on reasonable terms can be difficult because these projects require large up-front investments while the returns are reaped in the longer term. Experience to date indicates that prefinancing until output delivery is funded by the ESCOs (by definition of OBA), but longer-term ESCO financing has come from either government or multilateral sources (World Bank 2008b). In both Argentina and South Africa, the ESCO concessions received financing from provincial and federal government sources.

Grid connection projects leverage private capital mainly by working with private concessionaires. Leveraging can mean that private companies invest money complementary to OBA subsidies and user contributions (see box 5.3 on Senegal). Such investments are viable only if tariffs for poor beneficiaries are sufficient to cover ongoing costs and to pay back investments. Additionally, OBA can help mobilize upstream infrastructure by increasing the pool of customers serviced.

Monitoring

Outputs in OBA energy projects can include the installation (and sometimes maintenance) of SHSs or solar lanterns and, for grid-based technology, working connections to the energy network. In some cases, outputs include the provision of service over a period of months to ensure greater sustainability and demand. Monitoring and verification systems vary but often involve the appropriate line ministry for the energy sector in some capacity.

In Bangladesh's IDA-financed RERED off-grid project, IDCOL, the implementing agency, is responsible for ensuring verification of installations by dealers and maintaining a complete database on all SHS installations. Local officials such as schoolteachers are requested to undertake the initial checking of installations, which is followed up by inspections from a pool of inspectors and rechecking on a sample basis by IDCOL staff members. A technical group that handles certification of equipment that is eligible to be used in the program also supports IDCOL.

In Guatemala's grid-based PER, the technical committee, composed of representatives from both the ministry of energy and the concession companies, hires independent supervisors to verify that the connections made by the private distribution companies are eligible for reimbursement under the PER. The supervisors visit communities to check whether the new connections are outside the 200-meter zone and are in residential dwellings. They report to the ministry of energy, which sometimes performs additional checks. The ministry then submits a final report to the technical committee, which authorizes payment. As of May 2007, 189,383 connections had been completed and certified as operational, compared with the target of 280,000 connections. Funding for the remaining connections is uncertain because of the government's budgetary restrictions and delays in securing external funding.

For GPOBA projects, separate funding is provided to hire independent agencies to verify outputs. These agencies conduct random audits of connections installed and ensure that they meet the standards specified in the contract. In some cases, the verification agent is part of a government agency.

The monitoring and verification systems put in place for OBA schemes can be leveraged for broader purposes, however. OBA provides an opportunity for improved monitoring and evaluation, in particular for off-grid schemes in which this review can otherwise be very costly. For example, in the two Bolivian off-grid schemes, in which the providers and the verification agent are required to visit customers and report on the systems, the project implementation unit will receive information on the functioning of the systems, usage, and so forth.

Note

1. World Bank, REToolkit [Renewable Energy Toolkit], http://web.worldbank
.org/WBSITE/EXTERNAL/TOPICS/EXTENERGY2/EXTRENENERGY
TK/0,,menuPK:5138378~pagePK:149018~piPK:149093~theSitePK:513
8247,00.html.

## CHAPTER 6

Water and Sanitation

So far, the experience of output based aid (OBA) in the water sector is limited although the number of projects has grown dramatically in the last few years, the projects are at early stages and by and large small pilots. One of the reasons the water sector has relatively few OBA projects compared to the information and communication technology and energy sectors may be that OBA was originally set up as a public-private partnership mechanism, and the role of the private sector in formal water supply has been limited, especially after the retreat of international private water companies from developing countries after the 1990s. However, given a concerted effort to test OBA approaches in the water sector (including with public providers), as well as the emergence of an increasing number of regional and local private providers, some initial lessons can be shared.

Currently, 31 OBA projects in which the World Bank Group (WBG) participates are in the water and sanitation sectors. One additional OBA scheme was identified in the water sector outside the WBG. A large percentage of the funding value and number of projects are in Sub-Saharan Africa, in part because of the concerted efforts of the Global Partnership on Output-Based Aid (GPOBA) to pilot projects in that region (figure 6.1).

Figure 6.1   Regional Distribution of World Bank Group OBA Projects in Water and Sanitation

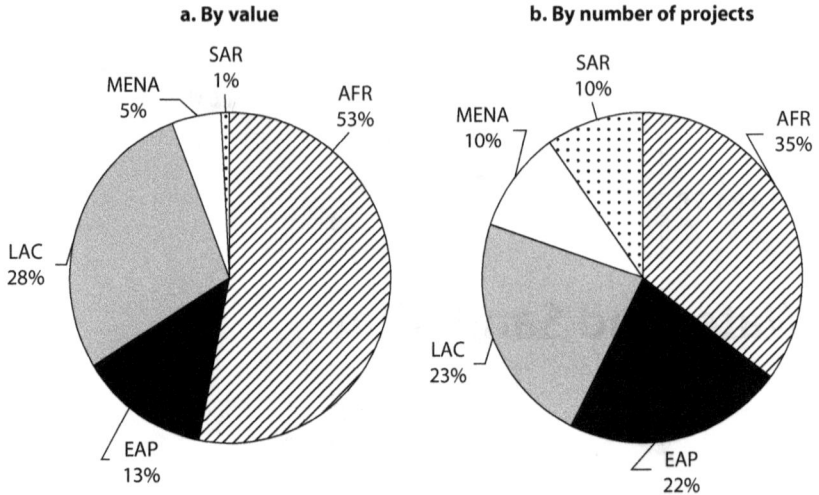

Source: GPOBA database.
Note: In panel a, total subsidy = US$169 million. In panel b, total projects = 31. AFR = Sub-Saharan Africa Region; EAP = East Asia and Pacific Region; LAC = Latin America and Caribbean Region; MENA = Middle East and North Africa Region; SAR = South Asia Region.

The majority of projects identified involve one-off subsidies for access. These projects involve piped-water schemes, and access is usually defined as the delivery of working connections as demonstrated through billing or collections. The majority of the projects are water supply projects, with about ten projects that involve either both water and sewerage or sanitation.

One project identified outside the WBG for the Chilean urban water sector involves ongoing lifeline subsidies. One closed project in Guinea funded by the International Development Association (IDA), Second Water Supply Project, involved transitional subsidies.

Funding

Of the 31 projects identified in the water and sanitation sectors, 9 include OBA subsidies funded by IDA and IBRD (International Bank for Reconstruction and Development), for a total WBG funding of US$105.6 million for the water sector.

Twenty projects include GPOBA subsidy funding for a total of US$63.3 million. Some of the GPOBA-funded schemes are part of a larger initiative by the IDA or the IBRD. Cofinancing was also provided in some cases by the government, the private sector, and, in a few cases, by the public sector utility (for example, the National Water and Sewerage Corporation in Kampala, Uganda).

In Honduras, a particularly innovative scheme involves setting up an OBA fund to target small and medium-size schemes, including green-field and brownfield projects in peri-urban and rural areas of the country. Funding sources include a contribution by the central government of US$1.0 million to provide bridge financing for subprojects being implemented by public operators with little or no access to commercial credit. GPOBA has provided US$4.4 million in grant funding. Other funding will come from the private operators, user contributions from a mixture of in-kind contributions and up-front payments (depending on the type of project), tariffs, standard sector contributions from the central government, or municipalities. In August 2008, the first subproject under the Honduran OBA facility was signed to implement a clean water project for 16 poor neighborhoods in Tegucigalpa, with a total population of over 53,000 expected to benefit. Currently, however, the project is on hold because of the country's political turmoil.

For the ongoing means-tested consumption subsidies in Chile's urban water sector, the subsidy scheme is funded entirely from the central government's budget. In 1998 alone, the subsidy scheme had a total cost of US$33.6 million and helped subsidize 450,000 households (Gómez-Lobo 2001).

Targeting

With a focus on access subsidies, OBA schemes in the water sector are inherently pro-poor because the poor are the most likely to lack connections to the supply network. However, other traditional mechanisms are used to ensure more effective targeting. Almost all of the water projects identified use geographic targeting as the primary mechanism. These water projects are usually small scale and located in geographic areas where the poorest groups are concentrated. In addition, a number of these projects use self-selection or means-tested targeting or both, which, in turn, increases their targeting effectiveness.

- The OBA in Kampala's Water Connections for the Poor project uses both geographic targeting and self-selection to provide access to piped-water services for poor households living in slum areas of Kampala.

The estimated approximate income level of the target population is less than US$1 per day per person. First outputs were delivered in March 2009, and as of July, more than 31,000 beneficiaries in the poorest areas of Kampala had been reached through 1,679 yard taps and 44 public water points.

- The Manila Water Supply project (box 6.1) uses a combination of geographic targeting and means-tested targeting. The project targets communities that are officially certified as indigent by standardized means proxy tests indicating that a majority of households fall under the national poverty line. The approximate per capita income of the target population is less than US$1 per day.

- The Improved Rural Community Water in Andhra Pradesh (India) project combines the three major targeting mechanisms—geographic,

Box 6.1

Manila Water Supply Project

The objective of the Manila Water Supply project is to increase access to water services through individual household connections by targeting low-income communities in the Manila Metropolitan Region. The Manila Water Company (MWC), the private Philippine company that provides water supply and sanitation services to approximately 5 million people in the East Zone of Metro Manila under a 25-year concession that began in 1997, is implementing the project. The concession has been operating successfully for over a decade, with a remarkable turnaround in service access (more than a 100 percent increase in number of connections), reliability (increase in 24-hour availability from 26 percent of customers to over 98 percent), water loss reductions (50 percent less loss), and overall operational efficiency.

The OBA scheme is building on MWC's considerable experience of working with low-income communities through its flagship program "Tubig Para Sa Barangay" (water for the community). Begun in 1998, the program has provided access to over 1 million low-income customers. MWC is investing about US$14 million in new water supply infrastructure in these areas, but the low-income households cannot afford the connection charges set by MWC and the regulator—currently 7,531.73 pesos (US$167). Under the OBA scheme, households contribute

(continued)

Box 6.1 *(Continued)*

1,620 pesos (US$36) toward the connection charge, and GPOBA provides a subsidy for the remainder. This unit subsidy is subject to annual indexation as specified in the terms of the concession contract. To make the household contribution more affordable, MWC has proposed an installment scheme over 12 months. The GPOBA subsidy is paid directly to MWC as a single payment, conditional on the independent verification of six months of satisfactory service delivery. The grant agreement was signed in October 2007. As of August 2009, a total of 10,642 water connections had been completed, of which 5,611 had been independently verified for satisfactory service provision for three months.

Sources: GPOBA database and authors.

means tested, and self-selection. The project aims to provide safe and affordable drinking water to about 12,500 households in 25 villages. These households purchase water in jerry cans from community water distribution points. To target individual beneficiaries in the villages, the project uses the government's white ration card, which entitles low-income individuals to obtain basic commodities (for example, rice or flour) at a reduced price (Mandri-Perrott 2008). As of August 2009, water treatment plants had been installed and independently verified in 20 villages, with the project overachieving its household targets already (15,476, compared with 12,500 planned), with only 20 of the 25 plants constructed and the rest expected to come online soon.

- Since the early 1990s, Chile has been successfully using an individual means-tested water consumption subsidy. Under the scheme, only means-tested households (based on a scoring system implemented by the government) are eligible for the lower-priced initial consumption block (15 cubic meters per month). This scheme has resulted in lower costs than the previous universal subsidy scheme and in higher targeting efficiency (Gómez-Lobo 2001).

Performance Risk

As in other sectors, the service provider under an OBA scheme in the water sector bears the risk of nonperformance—no reimbursement for costs incurred unless an output is verified. For the most part, outputs in the sector are defined as working connections, often demonstrated through billing or collection records. In most projects funded by GPOBA, a portion of the output-based payment is withheld until after several months of service delivery to enhance the sustainability of the scheme.

- In the Vietnam Rural Water project involving the East Meets West Foundation, an international nongovernmental organization, 80 percent of the subsidy is disbursed from GPOBA to the foundation upon realization of the connection and the remaining 20 percent after proof of six months of satisfactory service provision. By September 2009, 19 water schemes were operational with 8,759 verified household connections. More than 30 percent of these households have been independently verified for satisfactory water provision for six months.

- In Kenya's Microfinance for Small Water Schemes project, the community water associations are bearing performance risk because they will not be paid until they have provided evidence of outputs in the form of working connections and several months of service delivery, and, in some cases, demonstration of increased sales (box 6.2).

Box 6.2

Kenya Microfinance for Small Water Schemes

The Kenya Microfinance for Small Water Schemes project innovatively uses OBA subsidies to leverage commercial financing for up to 21 small rural and peri-urban piped-water systems in the country. Projects were selected from a wide pool that expressed interest through a district-level awareness campaign led by the Athi Water Services Board (regional asset-holding government agency). To qualify for the private microfinance bank's loans and the OBA subsidies, community projects must pass through K-Rep Bank's existing credit approval processes. The communities (organized into community associations) need to present their loan applications with considerable detail. For help in this process, the GPOBA-funded project has provided up-front technical assistance to communities, with considerable support from the multidonor Water and Sanitation Program. When a subproject loan is approved, K-Rep Bank is responsible for loan (and thus project) monitoring. The involvement of

(continued)

Box 6.2 *(Continued)*

a private lender with funds at risk increases oversight during project implementation and then ensures that systems are in place during operation, enhancing the sustainability of the subprojects.

Individual subprojects are financed through community equity (20 percent) and a loan provided by K-Rep Bank (80 percent). If the subproject meets the output targets—number of new connections and revenue collection—the output-based subsidy is released. The OBA subsidy covers 50 percent of the microfinance loan. The remainder of the loan is repaid through tariff revenue collection. The loan provided by K-Rep Bank is priced on a commercial basis and has a maximum tenor of five years. The OBA subsidy is believed to provide a degree of comfort to the bank. Hence, collateral requirements were less strenuous than usual, and the tenor was extended to five years over the normal one or two years. To provide additional security, K-Rep Bank has arranged a credit guarantee from the U.S. Agency for International Development through the Development Credit Authority for the life of the loan.

A grant provided by the Public-Private Infrastructure Advisory Facility is being used to develop a project development facility to assist communities in preparing loan applications. Furthermore, funding from the European Union Water Facility for developing countries in Africa, the Caribbean, and the Pacific is being used to increase the scale and scope of the project to a national level. As of August 2009, construction was under way for 8 of the 12 subprojects approved by K-Rep Bank. Construction has been completed and verified for two subprojects serving a total of 1,436 households.

Source: Virjee 2009.

- In the Jakarta water project described in box 6.3, outputs were both connections to the network and three months of billed consumption, with a minimum average consumption of 360 liters per day. The private operator, PT Pam Lyonnaise Jaya (PALYJA) is reimbursed on a sliding scale (depending on the proportion of targeted connections actually implemented) to incentivize the operator to go beyond the most easily reached targets.

As in other sectors (but possibly more acutely in the water sector given the reliance on small and local providers, nongovernmental organizations, and community organizations for service delivery), access to finance can be a binding constraint on the ability to prefinance outputs. This

Box 6.3

Expansion of Water Services in Low-Income Areas of Jakarta

The objective of this project is to increase piped-water access to poor urban and slum households in Jakarta through the incumbent operator, PALYJA. Majority owned by Suez Environnement, PALYJA has a 25-year water supply concession contract for western Jakarta and has been operational since 1997. The project uses output-based connection subsidies to connect low-income households that are located within larger areas that are already served (areas that are in the proximity of a secondary main). The project is able to provide services to poor urban households that would not be served because of their inability to afford the up-front connection charge. The OBA subsidy successfully transfers the performance risk to PALYJA with payment of 75 percent of the subsidy upon successful independent verification of the connection. The remaining 25 percent is paid after three months of satisfactory service delivery. Project construction began in mid-April 2008. As of August 2009, none of the 4,624 household connections made so far have been independently verified because the recruitment of the Independent Technical Auditor has not been finalized.

Sources: GPOBA database and authors.

constraint limits the performance risk that can be shifted to providers in these cases (see box 6.4 on the Water Supply in Uganda's Small Towns and Rural Growth Centers project currently being implemented).

Private Sector Capital and Expertise

The leveraging of private capital in the water sector is limited by the tariff charged to the targeted users because private financing leveraged is largely dependent on the investment costs being recovered through tariffs eventually. Traditionally, water tariffs have not been set high enough to cover large portions of investment. For example, in the Water Supply in Uganda's Small Towns and Rural Growth Centers project (box 6.4), the intention is to recoup 10 to 20 percent of the investments required for the scheme through the tariff. A larger amount would make tariffs unaffordable to the very households the OBA is intended to target.[1] In higher-income countries, however, leveraging might be higher.

Box 6.4

Phasing in Payments Because of Finance Constraints in Uganda's Water Sector

In the GPOBA-funded Water Supply in Uganda's Small Towns and Rural Growth Centers project involving small, local, private operators, two different output-based disbursement profiles were used. In small towns, where mainly extensions from the existing system were required, a relatively pure OBA is used whereby private operators will be paid after connections are completed and water service delivery is established. In the greenfield rural growth centers, however, output-based payments are phased so that 60 percent of the subsidies is disbursed during construction, and 40 percent of the subsidies is disbursed with final connections and water delivery. It was estimated that the availability and cost of financing until delivery of output, as well as the newness of the approach, would result in either very high bids that the poor population could not afford (because a portion of the costs would be borne through the tariff) or no bids. In subsequent batches, the output-based disbursement profile can possibly be more aggressive in the rural growth centers, but this plan will have to await the results of output delivery in the current pilot.

Ten initial lots have been bid out, resulting in at least 20 percent efficiency gains overall. Three of 10 towns did not require subsidies. Contracts were signed in October 2008, and output delivery began in the fourth quarter of 2008. As of August 2009, 552 yard-tap connections have been made (serving about 10,000 beneficiaries); 302 of these yard taps in two small towns have been independently verified.

Sources: GPOBA database and authors.

OBA schemes do allow the mobilization of private sector expertise to poor areas that the service provider might otherwise not have served. OBA schemes provide incentives for the extension of existing assets to serve poor households, provided the system has spare production capacity. Box 6.3 provides an example of how a large, international private operator is extending its services to poor areas in Jakarta through an OBA subsidy.

Monitoring

Outputs in the water sector mainly include functioning household, yard tap, or public kiosk connections to the network. In theory, the monitoring of outputs in the water sector is similar to that of other sectors. In practice, however, because the majority of water OBA schemes identified are funded by GPOBA and GPOBA tends to fund the hiring of independent verification agents, most water projects identified involve independent verification engineers that are hired through consultant contracts.

Because successful monitoring is key to learning lessons for future scale-up, government entities should also be involved. For example, in the Water Supply in Uganda's Small Towns and Rural Growth Centers project, the independent verification agent reports to the Directorate for Water Development of the Ministry of Water and Environment. Because of capacity issues in some cases, donor agencies may play a larger role in projects involving small and local providers.

The Morocco Urban Water and Sanitation project provides a good example of a more elaborate monitoring and verification system for an OBA scheme (box 6.5). However, one must note that Morocco has significant capacity, rated by the Organisation for Economic Co-operation

---

Box 6.5

Morocco Urban Water and Sanitation Project

As part of King Mohammed VI's National Initiative for Human Development, Morocco obtained a US$7 million grant from GPOBA to demonstrate OBA mechanisms to target sector funds and potential donor monies in support of the government of Morocco's challenge to extend water supply and sewerage service in recently legalized informal settlements in peri-urban areas. Two international private sector incumbents (Amendis in Tangiers and Lydec in Casablanca) and a public sector incumbent (Régie Autonome de Distribution d'Eau et d'Électricité de Meknès) are the service providers in their respective municipalities.

This OBA scheme has two levels of monitoring. As part of their progress reports, operators are to provide a quarterly monitoring report with information about the number of connections made, total number of beneficiary households, uptake rate of beneficiary households in each eligible area, average monthly consumption per beneficiary household, average expenditure on service by beneficiary households, and the collection rate for water bills and connection fees. This report is the basis for the independent verification of outputs-which also involves physically inspecting a random sample of outputs that lead to output-based payments.

(continued)

Box 6.5 *(Continued)*

A broader range of indicators is monitored on a yearly basis. Some indicators are static, and others require regular monitoring. Examples include an average residential tariff for beneficiary households; project unit costs of house connection operator and targeted area as per actual incurred expenditure; and discrepancies with estimated project costs. Additionally, service providers are encouraged to carry out yearly service-satisfaction surveys on a representative sample of about 10 percent of final beneficiaries.

As of August 2009, 3,353 water connections and 3,426 sewerage connections had been verified as delivered to prespecification standards.

Sources: GPOBA database and authors.

and Development as a "lower-middle income (or DAC 3) country," and because the service providers in two of the three subprojects are major international players.

Note

1. In the water supply in Uganda Small Towns and Rural Growth Centers pilot project, however, competitive tendering ultimately led to "zero subsidy bids" in a few towns, whereby the private operator plans to finance the costs of final connections wholly through the tariff that was set at bidding. This is a strong demonstration of private financing leveraged—although the results remain to be seen because the project has not closed.

CHAPTER 7

Health

Many traditional health schemes in developing countries work through a centralized government health system. As a result, the risk exists that decisions are made on a centralized level with little information about local conditions (for example, decisions on construction, equipment, and staffing of clinics, as well as procurement and distribution of medicine and other inputs). Centrally managed systems are complex; poorly aligned incentives and lack of information on local needs can result in a dearth of inputs, inadequate and poorly maintained infrastructure, and absenteeism of personnel. Using input-based health care systems also decreases transparency on who benefits from public funding. The *World Development Report 2004* highlights how the relatively wealthy benefit more from public spending than do the poor (World Bank 2003: 38ff).

Most countries have publicly funded health care systems; systems that rely exclusively on out-of-pocket payments are rare. Therefore, most health care systems already involve ongoing funding of service delivery. However, in reality, a lack of adequate public service in many poor countries means that large parts of the population (including the poor) end up paying a substantial share of their health expenditures out of pocket. Thus, OBA aims not so much to make additional subsidy funding available, but rather, to increase the efficiency of existing health care to expand access for greater coverage.

Output-based aid (OBA) is part of a larger universe of results-based financing (RBF) in the health sector. RBF involves payments to service providers (institutions such as hospitals and clinics), health care professionals, "payers" (for example, a government entity), or consumers when measurable actions are taken or defined performance targets are achieved. Although all OBA health contracts fall under the RBF umbrella, the reverse is not true: not all RBF contracts are OBA (see figure 7.1). For an RBF scheme to be considered OBA, it must meet two criteria:

- It involves a subsidy that covers the gap between the cost of providing a service and a price that is affordable to the user.
- Payments are linked to outputs, usually through some form of contractual arrangement that requires the contractor to bear at least a part of the performance risk of the intervention.

Figure 7.1   Universe of Results-Based Financing

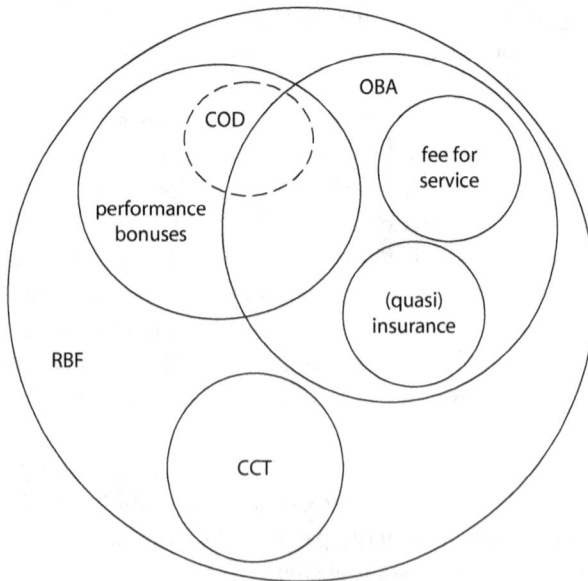

Source: Authors' representation.
Note: CCT = conditional cash transfer; COD = cash on delivery; OBA = output-based aid; RBF = results-based financing.

One example of an RBF instrument that is *not* OBA is the conditional cash transfer (CCT). CCTs are payments to households based on actions taken by the household, such as ensuring that children go to school or receive medical care. CCTs do not meet the definition of OBA because CCTs do not involve contracts with service providers and do not transfer risk to service providers by linking output delivery to subsidy disbursement. Thus, while OBA usually involves a "supply side" subsidy paid to the provider to incentivize it to deliver services, CCT focuses on "demand side" subsidies paid to final beneficiaries to incentivize them to seek these services (see box 7.1). Some other RBF instruments that may or may not be OBA, such as cash on delivery, are described in chapter 8 on the education sector.

Results-based mechanisms that pay a "fee for a service" or that provide coverage similar to health insurance generally meet the definition of OBA.[1] Other OBA designs in the health sector involve results-based contracts for the provision of service, for example, by nongovernmental

Box 7.1

Conditional Cash Transfers in the Social Services Sectors

CCT schemes focus on the demand side of health or education services by providing incentives for families to, for example, have their children immunized or send them to school. A CCT subsidy provided to the household promotes sending a child to a clinic (often distant) or helps a household invest in a child's education because these activities may have opportunity costs for the family (for example, taking time away from work on the family farm). These activities also may generate positive externalities to society (for example, vaccinations resulting in reduced disease) where benefits extend beyond the individual household level. CCT schemes differ from OBA because with CCTs, no performance risk exists for the supplier of services. Although different, OBA and CCT schemes can be complementary: CCT provides an incentive for the demand for health and education services, whereas OBA provides the incentive for the supply of health or education. Both are needed in the social services sectors in the poorest countries, where the direct benefits of services such as health and education are not always apparent to the poorest or hold a perceived high opportunity cost, and where providers are often in short supply to provide quality services. Further work needs to be done to explore how these different RBF instruments can work together to deliver better development outcomes.

organizations (NGOs) and can include the management of public facilities. Such projects usually involve block grants and performance bonuses conditional on achieving predefined performance indicators. Performance contracts between donors and governments or different levels of government can be OBA, if they involve bridging a gap between the cost of service delivery and affordability to the end user, paying for the provision of outputs, and transferring performance risks in a meaningful manner.

Projects can combine various results-based and output-based design elements. For example, Argentina's Maternal and Child Health Insurance Program (MCHIP), which provides health insurance to mothers and children in northern Argentina, combines a fee-for-service approach with performance indicators. Funded by the government of Argentina and the World Bank, the project pays per capita premiums to provincial insurance management agencies. A part of these payments is based on performance indicators, such as indicators for the effectiveness of prenatal care. As of January 2009, MCHIP had funded 115,000 deliveries and 1.5 million child medical consultancies, benefiting more than 527,000 people (almost 80 percent coverage of the eligible population in 2008). In 2007, a scale-up of the MCHIP (Phase II) began to extend coverage to the rest of the country and, as of February 2009, had successfully reached 388,118 beneficiaries.

The earliest output-based health schemes in developing countries were schemes to increase access to family planning in the Republic of Korea and Taiwan, China, in the early 1960s. The commitment to OBA schemes in the health sector by the World Bank Group over the past few years is an important example of the sector's drive for results. Currently, the portfolio of OBA health projects has reached US$863 million (figure 7.2). The majority of these projects are in the Latin America and the Caribbean and Sub-Saharan Africa Regions by value and in the Sub-Saharan Africa and South Asia Regions by number. The 2007 World Bank strategy for health, nutrition, and population calls for an increase in the "proportion of output-based lending in health" (World Bank 2007b: 27).

The following three principal archetypes of OBA contracts in the health sector have been identified:

- Performance-based contracts to provide health services
- Performance-based contracts to provide health insurance coverage
- Performance-based contracts to build or upgrade and maintain facilities or to accredit service providers and provide health services

Projects that directly provide health services to poor target groups, mainly by contracting out services to independent service providers such

Figure 7.2   Regional Distribution of World Bank Group OBA Projects in Health

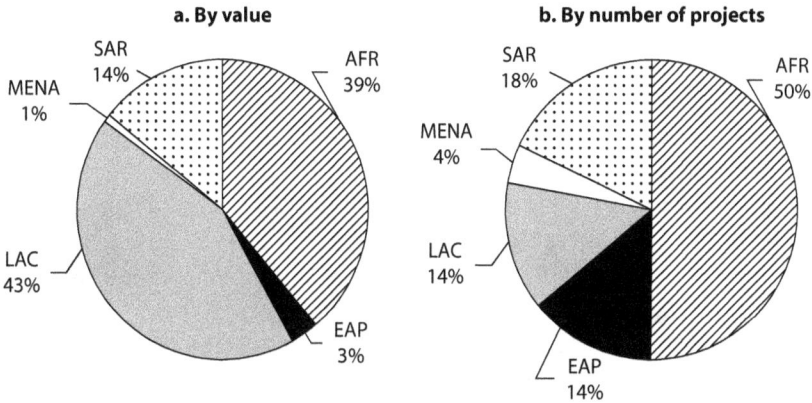

a. By value

b. By number of projects

Source: GPOBA database.
Note: In panel a, total subsidy = US$863 million. In panel b, total number of projects = 22. AFR = Sub-Saharan Africa Region; EAP = East Asia and Pacific Region; LAC = Latin America and Caribbean Region; MENA = Middle East and North Africa Region; SAR = South Asia Region.

as NGOs or local clinics, are the most common form of OBA in health. Projects providing beneficiaries with quasi-insurance coverage, for example, those that involve per capita transfers (capitations) from donors or central governments to an implementer, are increasingly being used, mainly in Latin America. Performance-based contracts with NGOs are used mainly when services must be rolled out in areas without existing infrastructure or service providers (for example, in postconflict areas) or where contractors take over service delivery from the public sector. Schemes working with multiple service providers, such as insurance or voucher projects, usually have a two-tier structure in which a project administrator (for example, a voucher management agency) has a performance contract with the project sponsor and individual service providers have contracts with the project administrator. In this case, service providers usually compete for patients and are reimbursed with a fixed fee for each intervention covered by the project. The only scheme identified in which a concessionaire rehabilitated and built facilities to provide health care service is a public-private partnership (PPP) hospital in Lesotho that involved Global Partnership on Output-Based Aid (GPOBA) subsidies (and the International Finance Corporation as transaction adviser; see box. 7.2). A GPOBA-funded project in the Philippines that is still in the design stage also aims to introduce an output-based scheme for upgrading and accreditation of small service providers.

Box 7.2

Lesotho New Hospital PPP

Lesotho's main public hospital and its most advanced medical institution—Queen Elizabeth II hospital—is more than 100 years old and performing poorly. The World Bank is supporting the design and implementation of a PPP for the replacement of the hospital and the inclusion of an OBA component. The International Finance Corporation was transaction adviser for this deal.

The project supports the design, construction, financing, and full operation of a hospital by a private partner for a contract period of 15 years. The project includes improvements to, and support for, the operation of two outpatient clinics associated with the hospital. A consortium led by Netcare, a South African health services company, was selected as the private operator. The hospital is expected to be fully operational in the fourth quarter of 2009.

Total construction costs are expected to reach US$72.5 million. Capital costs will be financed 20 percent by the private sector and 80 percent by the government of Lesotho. GPOBA will contribute a grant of US$6.25 million, payable over the first five years of the project, which will augment the government's payments.

The GPOBA subsidy aims to allow the following:

- More patients to be seen at a higher level of service at the filter clinics
- More patients to be seen at the new hospital and also at a higher level of service

Payments will be linked to volume and quality of service delivery. The Ministry of Health will conduct performance monitoring. Both the PPP hospital and filter clinics are currently under construction, and OBA service delivery is expected to start in the first half of 2010.

Sources: Ramatlapeng 2007; World Bank 2007c.

Funding

Because most health systems require ongoing subsidies for poor beneficiaries, projects rely on continued public support. The projects identified were funded mainly through government funds and international aid. Government funds can be raised through either general taxes or health care contributions (although the latter were not used for any of the identified projects).

Some projects require beneficiaries to make copayments, depending on their ability to pay. These contributions can be significant. For example, in the GPOBA Prepaid Health Scheme Pilot in Nigeria, beneficiaries pay a share of their insurance premium that increases over time—in total, approximately one-third of the cost of service. User contributions are frequently the means of gauging actual demand by the poor, even if the contributions are too small to add significantly to the funding of the project. (For example, the GPOBA Reproductive Health Vouchers in Western Uganda project charges US$1.71 for a safe delivery package with an average cost of US$72.00.)

Targeting

The identified projects use a number of different targeting instruments:

- At inception, most projects do not have sufficient resources to cover an entire country, so they use geographic targeting where subsidies are channeled to first reach the poorest locations.
- Most services offered by the identified projects are basic and usually involve basic health care facilities that are not attractive to the wealthier population (self-selection targeting).
- Some projects focus on marketing of services particularly to poor target groups (for example, targeting the sale of health vouchers to poor geographic areas).
- Projects providing both insurance and quasi-insurance can make eligibility for subsidy contingent on the beneficiaries not being covered by other health insurance (self-selection targeting).
- The most effective method of targeting, but also the most expensive to implement, is the assessment of household income (means testing) or the use of indicators to estimate household wealth (proxy means testing).

The identified projects either rely primarily on one targeting mechanism or combine several mechanisms to improve targeting efficiency:

- The first component of the Health Sector Rehabilitation Support project of the Democratic Republic of Congo (DRC) targets 67 of the DRC's 513 health zones (World Bank 2005b). The second component of the project targets 89 health zones (16.4 percent of the DRC's population) that have the worst health indicators and little or no donor and government support.

- The Reproductive Health Vouchers in Western Uganda project, which builds on a pilot project funded by KfW (Kreditanstalt für Wiederaufbau) and is itself cofunded by KfW, works with very basic midwife-operated private health centers in rural areas in the greater Mbarara region. Eligibility for participating in the voucher scheme is determined by mobile voucher sales agents using a proxy means-testing questionnaire to determine living conditions as a proxy for household income. The first OBA healthy baby was delivered on February 28, 2009. As of September 2009, 246 babies had been safely delivered.
- In Argentina, anybody working for the formal sector is already covered by health insurance. The MCHIP is targeted exclusively to women and children who do not have access to formal insurance.

Performance Risk

The identified health projects transfer varying degrees of risk to service providers. When service providers are paid a fee for services performed, they must first invest in infrastructure and equipment to perform services. They have to purchase inputs (such as medicine) and staff their health centers to provide services. If they are unable to provide services at a cost below the defined reimbursement, they stand to lose money. At the same time, they have to provide services at a level to meet pre-agreed quality standards and attract patients. (The latter is particularly important in projects with multiple service providers that compete for patients.) Individual service providers may be able to mitigate part of the prefinancing risk by first using spare capacity in existing facilities and then gradually expanding capacity. Contractors with a concession to roll out services in previously underserved or unserved areas typically incur a larger up-front investment and thus can be at greater risk. This risk is typically mitigated by providing part of the subsidy as a block grant, complemented by an output-based payment for reaching a number of indicators of pre-agreed service quality, level, or outcome.

Some evidence indicates that the freedom to allocate funds under a block grant combined with close monitoring of results (and the implicit threat of discontinuing contracts) imposes discipline on contractors. A controlled study of three groups of service providers in Uganda (receiving input-based funding, block grants, and block grants with performance bonuses, respectively) showed significantly poorer performance of service providers under input-based financing, but no significant difference between the two groups that were free to use block grants how they deemed best (Johannes and others 2008). The implications of these findings are not clear. Several factors may be contributing to the explanation: an intrinsic motivation to deliver good results, an insufficient amount of bonuses, or the NGOs' awareness that their performance was to be scrutinized under the study and their fear that poor performance could affect their future ability to raise funds.

Another way of paying for results is used under the DRC's Health Sector Rehabilitation Support project, where NGOs enter into performance-based contracts with individual health zone administrations and facilities. Such contracts usually set performance indicators, including immunization coverage or outpatient consultation targets. Health worker incentives are tied to performance on a list of indicators, often summarized by a single score. The health indicators include numbers of outpatient visits, malaria treatments given to children, child immunizations, prenatal visits, and attended births.

- In Rwanda under the Poverty Reduction Support Credit II, health centers are reimbursed for the quantity of services provided according to a standardized fee structure for 14 services, adjusted by a composite quality score. Hospital budgets are based on an average annual value per bed. Participating service providers are at risk of not being reimbursed if they are unable to attract patients and of losing money if they are unable to provide services of the required quality at a cost below scheduled reimbursement.

- In 2003, the World Bank began the Health Sector Emergency Reconstruction and Development project in Afghanistan (World Bank 2006a). Part of this scheme was the Extension and Expansion of the Basic Package of Health Services project, through which the Ministry of Public Health signs performance-based partnership agreements with NGOs that are competitively selected. The NGOs receive performance bonuses worth 10 percent of their contracts if they perform satisfactorily on 10 health indicators. The ministry contracted Johns Hopkins University to evaluate the performance of the NGOs.

- The original KfW-funded voucher project treating sexually transmitted diseases in rural Uganda mainly worked with small health posts and clinics run and operated by nurses and midwives. A well-designed billing system that ensures rapid reimbursements helped service providers mitigate issues of access to finance by gradually expanding the facilities and the range of services provided.

Private Sector Capital and Expertise

For fee-for-service arrangements, service providers are usually expected to bear the entire investment costs, to be recouped through fee reimbursements. Some assistance may be made available to help facilities meet the accreditation criteria. Contracting out basic service delivery can require larger investments by the recipient and thus can involve block grants to reduce the need for private investments. In such cases contracting with the private sector can mainly have the objective to mobilize private expertise.

The amount of up-front capital investment also varies for different service levels to be provided. Projects involving secondary and tertiary care that require specialized facilities and equipment are more capital intensive than those concentrating on primary care delivery – as in the case of the Lesotho Hospital PPP described earlier in box 7.1. On the other hand, a number of highly effective primary care interventions can be delivered without the need for specialized facilities or other up-front investments, and primary care interventions can more easily rely on existing basic medical infrastructure and spare capacity in existing private service providers.

Monitoring

As described earlier, outputs for OBA schemes in the health sector vary greatly, from insurance schemes to actual in-hospital deliveries, immunizations, HIV testing, and so forth. In the projects identified earlier, monitoring and evaluation (M&E) were performed by government agencies, NGOs, the private sector, or self-reporting. Table 7.1 gives examples of projects that use each of these groups to perform M&E.

In many cases, projects use a combination of different M&E mechanisms. For example, in the DRC's Health Sector Rehabilitation Support project (World Bank 2005b), M&E functions are contracted out to the private sector and carried out by government agencies and NGOs.

Some health sector OBA projects use demographic and health surveys to monitor and evaluate project success, usually when projects target a large portion of a country or region's population. For example, in Argentina's first

Table 7.1   Parties Responsible for M&E in Contracts to Provide Health Services

Party performing M&E	Example
Government agency	In Argentina's two Provincial Maternal-Child Health Investment projects, the National Health Services Purchasing Team is responsible for monitoring project coverage. Service providers collect data on provinces and provider performance as they record the service deliveries that form the basis for their payments. The national team consolidates the data and evaluates it against the tracer goals from the Annual Performance Agreements. The national team and the Provincial Health Services Purchasing Team also conduct periodic independent audits of the data, including surveys of beneficiary participation and satisfaction.
NGO	In the DRC's health zone system, health service providers self-report on the services they deliver. These services are then verified by the NGOs with which the service providers contract.
Private sector contractor	A large portion of M&E in the DRC's Health Sector Rehabilitation Support project is contracted out to a private sector firm.
Self-reporting	Self-reporting is used in a number of projects, but self-reported results are always verified or audited by third parties. Projects in which self-reporting is used include the DRC's health zone system, Argentina's two Provincial Maternal-Child Health Investment projects, and Paraguay's Mother and Child Basic Health Insurance project.

Source: GPOBA database.

Provincial Maternal-Child Health Investment projects, data on baseline state of tracers were generated by the baseline study being implemented nationwide. This study included both data gathered from provider-based information systems and household panel surveys that include biological impact markers.

Projects working on a fee-for-service basis frequently rely on monitoring mechanisms designed to ensure service quality and adherence to service standards in addition to the verification of a sample of individual interventions. Such measures can include a periodic review of facilities to make sure they meet accreditation standards, review of documentation to audit the adherence to treatment protocols, and, in some cases, mystery patients who anonymously test the quality of services delivered.

A recent article in *The Lancet* reports that a research team found significant differences between vaccination figures reported by beneficiaries of the Global Alliance on Vaccines and Immunization as determined through independent surveys (Lim and others 2008). This difference "suggests that … [the Global Alliance on Vaccines and Immunization] may have paid out twice as much in performance rewards as it should have: [US]\$290 million instead of [US]\$150 million" (Brown 2008). Even if, as suggested by the Center for Global Development,[2] part of this difference can be explained by statistical biases (such as a tendency of surveys to underreport vaccination data), this incident highlights the necessity for a combination of a robust M&E system and independent verification of outputs.

Notes

1. These mechanisms include schemes in which public institutions provide coverage similar to an insurance mechanism except that they usually are publicly managed and cannot decline to enroll individuals. In some cases, participation in such schemes is compulsory.

2. Center for Global Development. "Global Health Policy" blog. http://blogs.cgdev .org/globalhealth/2008/12/new-lancet-article-about-gavi.php.

## CHAPTER 8

Education

Output-based aid (OBA) in education is used to bridge a gap between the cost of providing quality education and the funds available. It usually involves payments to schools based on predefined outputs, such as enrollment and attendance of specified school-age children, and often includes school achievement as a performance indicator.

OBA approaches in the education sector are limited in number. This review identified five OBA schemes in the World Bank Group that provide performance-based grants for the actual delivery of education services. These include two Female Secondary School Assistance Projects (FSSAPs) in Bangladesh, the Lifelong Learning and Training Project in Chile, and the Balochistan Education Support Project in Pakistan, all funded by the World Bank. One output-based education project funded by the Global Partnership on Output-Based Aid (GPOBA), aiming to support upper secondary education in Vietnam, is currently under preparation. Additionally, the review identified a government-funded project in Colombia. The scale of subsidy disbursements ranged from US$2.1 million for the scheme in Balochistan to over US$100 million in Chile and over US$135 million for the two phases in Bangladesh. Two of the schemes aimed at improving student enrollment and attendance, and quality of education, and one provided learning opportunities for adults. All schemes used extensive government cofunding.

However, together with OBA, a variety of other results-based schemes exist in the education sector. They include conditional cash transfers, described in box 7.1 of chapter 7, and cash on delivery (COD), described in box 8.1.

Funding

Funding for the identified OBA schemes comes from a variety of sources: IDA, IBRD, government revenues, parent contributions, and private investments. The US$232.6 million for Bangladesh's FSSAP was a combination of IDA and government money, and the community contributed US$200,000 (box 8.2). In Chile's Lifelong Learning and Training Project, the IBRD matched the US$75 million contribution of the government of Chile with a loan. The GPOBA-funded project in Vietnam expects to provide US$3 million in subsidies. Some projects require that parents contribute toward the tuition cost to complement the outside funding. The project targeting private schools in Balochistan, which are generally believed to offer higher-quality education than public schools, requires such contributions.

Targeting

The OBA educational schemes in developing countries aim mainly at targeting services to low-income households. The schemes tend to use

---

Box 8.1

Cash on Delivery

Cash on delivery, or COD, is a results-based scheme proposed by the Center for Global Development to improve results in the education sector. The center proposes to pay the recipient government a predetermined amount for a certain measure of progress without prescribing the means or policy to achieve it. The scheme does not address a specific funding gap; rather, it is an incentive payment to a government for a specific output. For example, donors could promise to pay a certain amount for every additional child who completes his or her primary education and sits for a test. COD would involve hands-off unconditional payments. This review has not identified any COD projects under implementation.

Source: Birdsall and others 2008.

Box 8.2

Bangladesh's Female Secondary School Assistance Project

The two phases of Bangladesh's Female Secondary School Assistance Project aimed at increasing school enrollment and attendance of female students and improving the quality of secondary education. FSSAP I provided stipends to female students in grades 6–10 attending at least 75 percent of the school year and obtaining annual examination marks of at least 45 percent. Originally, stipends amounted to US$18 to US$45 per student per year but were reduced to US$5 to US$16 by 2001 to accommodate more students. The stipends and tuition were to cover full tuition and board; examination costs; and an increasing proportion of school fees, textbooks, stationery, uniforms, shoes, and transport. The tuition fees were disbursed to schools, while the stipends were paid to the female students.

Over the life of FSSAP I, enrollment of female students in supported schools more than doubled, and overall, about 1.6 million girls received stipends. (The program funded 4.9 million girl-years compared to a planned 3.32 million girl-years.) FSSAP II largely followed the OBA approach of its predecessor. It funded 6.9 million girl-years of education (compared to a planned number of 6.3 million girl-years).

Sources: Implementation Completion Reports.

means testing or proxy means testing, as well as geographic targeting. Geographic targeting is particularly common where projects are small and confined to a specific geographic area. For example, new private schools in Balochistan were opened when no other school operated within a 2-kilometer radius and were required to enroll at least 40 percent female students. In countries where the literacy gap between male and female students is significant, the OBA schemes can specifically target girls. For example, the districts for Bangladesh's FSSAP were identified on the basis of their economic level of development, low female literacy rates, and low female attendance levels.

Some schemes use existing means-testing or proxy means-testing systems to avoid subsidizing wealthier students already enrolled in private schools. For example, the Concession Schools program specifically targets marginalized low-income areas of Bogotá in need of school spaces. The Lifelong Learning and Training Project in Chile relies on self-selection and targeted marketing to provide vocational training to adults ages 15–65, because vocational training is usually more attractive to the poorer segments of the population.

Performance Risk

The challenge of introducing OBA in education has often been defining the appropriate output that is closely linked with the desired outcomes without putting efficient service providers at too much risk. For example, paying only on enrollment may be considered insufficient incentive for providing quality education; at the same time, the extent to which subsidy disbursements (payments to providers) can be tied to academic achievements is somewhat limited, since academic achievement is not fully under the control of the service provider. As a result, a project could disburse on a combination of attendance and measures of the quality of education:

- In Pakistan, the government of Balochistan promotes low-fee, good-quality primary private education by disbursing annual subsidies per student for facilities and material costs to the agency that manages the private schools established under the World Bank project and a monthly subsidy linked to student enrollment and attendance.
- Under the Concession Schools program in Bogotá, private school operators manage public schools and are responsible for meeting the preestablished targets on standardized tests and dropout rates for two consecutive years to qualify for state funding.
- In the Lifelong Learning and Training Project in Chile, the performance risk is borne by the private service provider who is paid on the basis of a student's demonstrated completion of a learning module.
- The GPOBA Vietnam education project proposes to disburse a part of tuition fees as subsidies to private and semi-public schools, on the basis of students attending at least 80 percent of classes and having a passing score on tests.

One well-known form of OBA in education is the voucher scheme, in which parents choose schools based on perceived quality of education. Although no discernible effect of vouchers on the overall quality of education could be found in Chile, vouchers have led to a more competitive market for schools in some European countries.

Private Sector Capital and Expertise

In most countries, education is largely provided by public schools and financed publicly. The private sector capital and expertise in education are used in various ways and can be split into two main categories: (a) the building and maintaining of infrastructure and (b) the provision of education services (teaching). Private sector capital is mainly mobilized to build, operate, and maintain education infrastructure. Projects can also, to some extent, rely on existing infrastructure (for example, through vouchers that pay for additional students in existing private schools).

As box 8.3 demonstrates, private sector involvement can in some cases effectively address issues related to quality of education and school management. In developing countries, where scarce government resources cannot provide education for all, partnering with the private sector may be a solution. The inclusion of low-fee private schools in the Balochistan Educational Support Project followed the successful implementation of a pilot phase in which private schools supplied low-cost, high-quality education for female students from very poor urban areas of the province.

Box 8.3

Impact of Private Sector Participation in the Concession Schools Program in Bogotá

The public-private partnership in Bogotá was created to provide education to 45,000 students from low-income neighborhoods and serves as evidence of the positive impact of private sector involvement on attendance and school attainment. The program is based on a bidding process in which the applicant must demonstrate previous experience in the education sector. To qualify for state funding, the winning private school operators are responsible for meeting preestablished targets on standardized tests and dropout rates for two consecutive years. The following encompasses the impact of the program:

- First, the freedom to choose the teaching and administrative staff in the private institutions can lead to better control of the quality of education. On average, 55 percent of the subsidy amount was allocated to human resources, well below the 90 percent amount in the public school system, freeing 33 percent for nutritional support and education materials.
- Second, the eligibility of private operators for continued support depends on meeting preestablished standardized test scores, which emphasizes the importance of higher-quality education rather than merely good school operation.
- Third, private sector providers are incentivized to partner with parents and the community, which helped reduce the dropout rates and improve educational attainment, compared to regular public schools.

Source: Barrera-Osorio 2006.

The private schools selected by the project receive an annual per student subsidy for facilities and material costs and a monthly subsidy linked to student enrollment and attendance.

Monitoring

To make payment on outputs feasible, one must define outputs in a measurable and discrete manner. Such outputs can include enrollment, attendance, or educational attainment, which may be measured by standardized tests. Schools themselves, government entities, consultancy firms, or nongovernmental organizations can undertake monitoring. Projects based on school choice rely on parents to judge the quality of schools in which they enroll their children. Data gathered as part of output verification can provide feedback to inform education policy (for example, during periodic reviews of curricula).

Monitoring systems for OBA projects in education must be carefully designed. Self-reporting of enrollment or attendance may provide an incentive to inflate output figures, and standardized tests have a risk of providing an incentive for "teaching to the test"[1] and for cheating to secure funding. Independent verification can help ensure that subsidies are paid only for outputs that have been achieved. If government institutions verify outputs, such institutions must be sufficiently independent and have sufficient capacity. For mitigation of the risk of teaching to the test and cheating, the Center for Global Development's concept of COD (see box 8.1) proposes tying incentive payments to student participation in standardized testing—but not to test results. Instead, the results of tests would be made available to the public so that parents could insist on quality improvements in schools achieving below-average results.

Note

1. Questions in a standardized test can be only an imperfect proxy for the skills they are supposed to measure. *Teaching to the test* means that teachers focus on teaching a narrow skill set they may deem necessary to solve questions they anticipate a test could ask. The result could be deteriorating standards of education, even if test scores improve. This is one of the criticisms of standard-based reform such as the No Child Left Behind Act in the United States.

## PART III

Cross-Cutting Lessons

## CHAPTER 9

Cross-Cutting Lessons Learned: Challenges and Best Practice

This chapter analyzes the output-based aid (OBA) portfolio against the benchmarks and criteria that were set out at the early stages of piloting as purported advantages of OBA. These benchmarks and criteria include the following:

- *Increased transparency through the explicit targeting of subsidies,* tying these subsidies to defined outputs
- *Increased accountability by shifting performance risk to service providers* by paying them after they have delivered an agreed output
- *Increased engagement of private sector capital and expertise* by encouraging the private sector to serve customers (usually the poor) they might otherwise disregard
- *Encouragement of innovation and efficiency* by leaving the service "solutions" partly up to the service provider and through least cost determination of the subsidy required
- *Increased sustainability of public funding* by allowing one-off subsidies and linking ongoing subsidies to sustainable service
- *Enhancement of monitoring* of results because payments are made against agreed outputs

In judging the merits of OBA, this book aims to answer the following two questions: (a) to what extent do OBA projects meet the six criteria listed above, and (b) does OBA fulfill these criteria better than traditional aid approaches? For an answer to the first question, most lessons are drawn from the World Bank Group (WBG) portfolio of 34 closed projects and 78 projects under implementation, most of which are delivering outputs. Lessons are also drawn to some extent from the 19 WBG projects at design stage and from non-WBG projects for which sufficient information is available. Figure 9.1 depicts the percentage breakdown of WBG OBA projects by stage of project development.

As to the second question, the main challenge is establishing a valid counterfactual: to allow conclusions about the relative effectiveness of OBA, one must compare OBA projects to projects with similar objectives but using other approaches. The difficulty in doing so is that, because no two projects are totally alike, comparing unit costs, for example, across projects may be meaningless.[1] Nevertheless, comparing OBA with a sufficiently large sample of similar (but not the same) traditional projects could lead to some interesting results. However, the availability of data for traditional projects is limited. Nevertheless, some studies were found that can put OBA in the context of other aid modalities. For example, on the targeting incidence of utility subsidies and the pro-poor benefits of connection subsidies such as those that are predominant with OBA, see Komives and others (2005).

Figure 9.1   WBG OBA Projects by Project Status

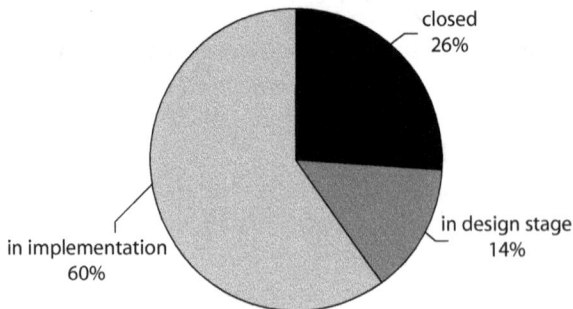

Source: GPOBA database.
Note: Total number of projects = 131.

Transparency: Explicit Targeting of Subsidies for the Poor

The review conducted to date concludes that OBA provides a stronger platform from which to target infrastructure and social services subsidies than do traditional interventions in these sectors. First, the access focus of OBA schemes can help ensure limited subsidies are reaching those who most need them. Second, explicit targeting linking subsidies to specific users and uses is common across all the sectors where OBA is prevalent—except for the roads sector and to a limited extent the ICT sector, where the public good (access for all) nature makes exclusively targeting the poor difficult. Third, the process of output verification also inherent in OBA schemes provides an additional check on the accurate targeting of subsidies and helps provide early evidence that OBA schemes are reaching the poor.

Subsidies Aimed at Improving Access

Traditional input-based schemes that subsidize specific investment projects such as power plants or more general budget support for utilities are often equivalent to across-the-board subsidies, because they decrease the tariffs needed to cover costs. Because wealthier households tend to consume more utility services than do poorer households, the bulk of such subsidies benefit nonpoor households. Furthermore, a large percentage of the poor are often not connected to such network services in the first place and so cannot benefit from these across-the-board subsidies.

Quantity-based tariff subsidies that charge lower tariffs for lower quantities of water or electricity are a common method of attempting to target utility subsidies to the poor.[2] However, empirical evidence from the water and electricity sectors shows that such subsidies usually lead to regressive targeting because of:

- Exclusion of the (overwhelmingly poor) households not connected to the network
- Fixed charges that negate subsidy benefits if they increase effective average tariffs of low-consumption households
- Increasing block tariffs that subsidize first units consumed by all income strata, whether rich or poor and regardless of total consumption behavior
- In some cases, low social tariffs that result in incentives to increase the upfront connection costs for users as compensation for lost revenue through the tariff subsidy (Komives and others 2005: 79ff)

- Lack of clear correlation between income and consumption in some sectors, such as water (Komives and others 2005: 82ff, 167)

OBA in the infrastructure sectors mainly relies on one-off capital subsidies for increased access—usually through connection, in network industries. These OBA subsidies aim to increase access to poor households in the first instance. Then, if quantity-based subsidies are implicit in the system, poor households can also benefit from them, provided the quantity-based subsidies are properly designed to actually benefit the poor.[3]

In the social sectors, traditional funding mechanisms may not primarily benefit the poorer segments of the population. "[W]hile governments devote about a third of their budgets to health and education, they spend very little of it on poor people—that is, on the services poor people need to improve their health and education. Public spending on health and education is typically enjoyed by the non-poor" (World Bank 2003: 3). For example, the poor frequently live in areas with little or no access to health care services (such as rural areas and poor neighborhoods). They are less able to wield political influence to direct health care spending to these areas and the basic services they need most urgently. Furthermore, the usual form of funding hospitals and health centers benefits all patients and all types of interventions. When buildings, drugs, machines, and salaries are subsidized, all users benefit, regardless of whether they require basic emergency care or less-urgent, upscale procedures. OBA subsidies, however, often through ongoing subsidy mechanisms, target services the poor are more likely to use. Several OBA schemes in the health and education sectors help mitigate the cost of access to poor households as well (for example, the quasi-insurance schemes in Latin America).

Sharpening Traditional Forms of Targeting with OBA
All OBA schemes by definition must specify the outputs against which subsidies will be disbursed. Consequently, beneficiaries can be identified more clearly than in traditional input-based schemes. An analysis of the OBA portfolio to date describes the following forms of targeting used in OBA schemes, examples of which have been provided in detail in the sector-specific chapters 3 through 8:

- *Geographic targeting.* Most OBA projects use geographic targeting. This form of targeting is useful when intended beneficiaries are concentrated in certain areas and few people outside the target group live there. For projects in such areas, excluding unintended beneficiaries can be costlier than including them. Geographic targeting is more complicated and less effective in areas where the poor and the non-poor live relatively interspersed.

- *Self-selection targeting.* This form of targeting involves designing projects to ensure that outputs chosen by poorer beneficiaries receive a higher share of subsidies. Subsidies can be targeted progressively by providing higher subsidies for more basic services or by subsidizing services less attractive to the rich. For example, because wealthier patients tend to favor more sophisticated upmarket facilities, OBA projects usually finance more basic health care services. Many OBA projects have used self-selection to complement geographic targeting (see box 9.1).

- *Means-testing targeting.* Several OBA schemes, particularly those in middle-income countries, use this type of targeting. Means testing

---

Box 9.1

Nepal's Biogas Support Program: Geographic Plus Self-Selection Targeting

The Biogas Support Program in rural Nepal provides household-size biogas plants to families. Biogas plants use decomposition of organic waste, such as cow manure, to produce a flammable gas that can be used for cooking and lighting. The subsidies vary according to the plant's size and location. Smaller plants, used by poorer families, receive relatively higher subsidies than larger plants. Wealthier families, with more livestock to provide input, prefer larger plants with greater gas output. Plants in remote mountainous regions, where the population is poorer, receive a higher subsidy than plants in the Terai lowlands, where the population is richer. The higher subsidy for remote mountainous regions is also meant to offset the higher related construction costs. The Biogas Support Program has successfully installed over 150,000 biogas plants funded by the Netherlands Directorate-General for International Cooperation, Germany's KfW, and the Community Development Carbon Fund. As of August 2009, 9,227 biogas plants had been installed under a GPOBA-funded component, of which 4,772 plants have been independently verified.

involves measuring a beneficiary's wealth to assess whether a subsidy is warranted. Such schemes require more advanced administrative systems. For this reason, OBA schemes that rely on means testing usually piggyback on broader welfare programs that identify poor households for a variety of public services (see examples in chapter 5 for Armenia and Colombia gas projects). One approach used by some OBA projects includes *proxy means testing*, in which easily observable characteristics, such as possession of indicative assets (for example, a dwelling of a certain size), are used as a proxy for income.

- *Community-based targeting.* This type of targeting relies on collaboration with the local community or its representatives to help identify the community members most in need of the service. Community involvement can increase ownership and reduce the risk that the population in the service area rejects targeting criteria. However, community-based targeting may have drawbacks, such as the risk of being hijacked by special interests. Moreover, this form of targeting can be time consuming, as evidenced by the Water Access with Small-Scale Providers project in Cambodia (Navarro and Tavarez 2008).

Information on the targeting mechanism used could be identified for 101 of 131 projects (see figure 9.2).[4] About two-thirds of these OBA schemes used geographic targeting, 24 percent used self-selection targeting, and 11 percent used means testing. Several projects used more than one targeting methodology in combination.

Ultimately, the choice of targeting mechanism for any OBA scheme will depend on several factors, mainly the nature of service delivery in the sector; cost-benefit considerations (see table 9.1); and the existing enabling environment, particularly the type of social welfare mechanisms already in place and the ability to appropriately monitor them.

A combination of geographic and self-selection targeting seems to be the most promising methodology for OBA in lower-income countries, whereas income-, proxy means-, and means-testing targeting seem more appropriate in the middle-income or lower-middle-income (IBRD and blend) countries within which the WBG operates.

Role of Output Verification for Targeting

Eligibility criteria for beneficiary households are usually clearly defined and made a precondition for subsidy disbursements. The third-party verification that triggers disbursement of OBA funds can sometimes include verification that the poverty-targeting criteria have been met.

Figure 9.2   Targeting Mechanisms in OBA Projects

a. Targeting mechanisms

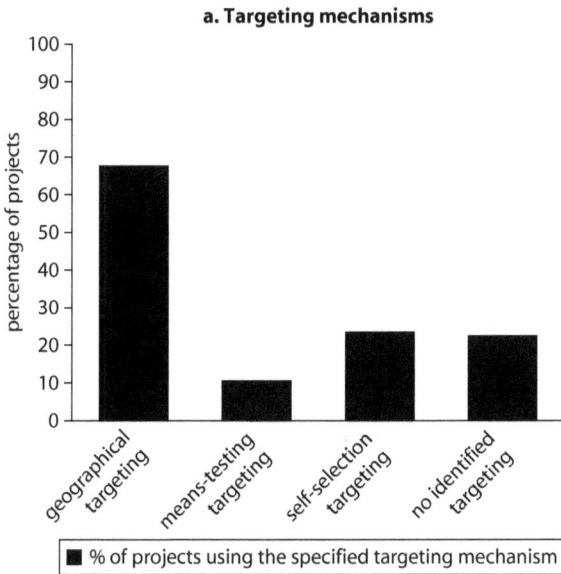

b. Distribution of projects with no identified targeting mechanism by sector

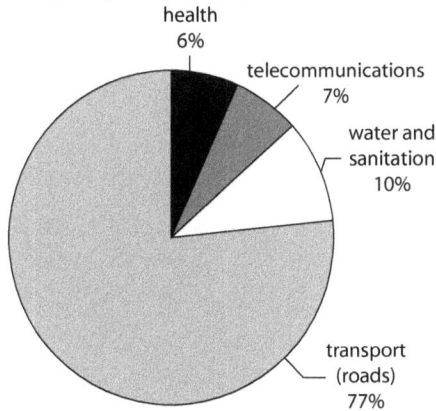

Source: GPOBA database.

- Voucher schemes in health can be used to market services specifically to the poor (for example, by selling vouchers in poor areas or targeting social marketing campaigns to high-risk groups). Verification of targeting can be included in voucher schemes by making vouchers nontransferable (for example, by registering biometric data of voucher recipients).

Table 9.1   Cost and Effectiveness of Targeting Mechanisms

Targeting approach	Cost and administrative complexity	Targeting effectiveness
Geographic	Low	Low to moderate
Self-selection	Low	High
Means testing	High	High
Proxy means testing	Moderate	Moderate
Community-based	Moderate to high	Moderate

Sources: GPOBA; Grosch and others 2008.

- In projects using geographic targeting, output verification occurs only in preidentified low-income areas.
- For projects using self-selection targeting, verification that the correct outputs are delivered (for example, outdoor yard taps versus indoor water connections) usually implies verification of targeting.

The output verification process inherent in OBA schemes does not necessarily lead to foolproof targeting, but if verification is reliable and robust, it can enhance targeting substantially (see "Monitoring of Results" section later in this chapter).

Accountability: Shifting Performance Risk to Providers[5]

OBA schemes shift performance risk to the service provider by paying the service provider *after* the delivery of prespecified outputs. More specifically, the components of performance risk that are shifted to the service provider to a greater extent through OBA mechanisms than through traditional input-based schemes include the following (depending on the sector and the nature of the subsidy mechanism):

- Construction risk related to infrastructure and other investments made under the project, particularly the risk of cost overruns or benefit shortfalls caused by nondelivery of outputs or delivery of inappropriate or insufficient outputs
- Operational risk related to ongoing service delivery
- Demand risk (or uptake risk) related to whether the intended beneficiaries request the service provided at the price provided

By shifting performance risk to service providers, OBA can raise some additional unintended risks, in particular, the payment risk that after outputs have been prefinanced and delivered as agreed, subsidy disbursements (or payments to the provider) are substantially delayed or not made. OBA design must incorporate measures to mitigate for this potential risk.

OBA schemes could result in higher unit costs for the service provider and therefore higher charges for the user, since the provider would be taking on more risk through an OBA scheme compared to a similar input-based scheme—although this must be weighed against the probability and related costs of nondelivery through more input-based approaches. No evidence to date indicates that OBA schemes are more costly than their input-based counterparts—in fact, more evidence exists to the contrary. Given the increased risk taken on by providers under OBA schemes, however, further evidence (through, for example, impact evaluations) is required, along with more quantification of the economic and social cost of nondelivery using traditional input-based schemes as comparators.

Construction Risk and One-Off Subsidies

A large number of sources provide anecdotal evidence that cost overruns and benefit shortfalls occur frequently in international aid projects and infrastructure projects in general. Nevertheless, very few systematic studies exist that can be used to compare results with the sample of OBA projects that are under implementation or already completed. Flyvbjerg (2005) gives a number of examples for cost overruns in infrastructure. In another article, Flyvbjerg, Holm, and Buhl (2002) find that of 258 transport projects, 86 percent exceeded cost expectations with an average overrun of 28 percent.

OBA can help mitigate some of the risk of cost overruns (or benefit shortfalls) related to project investments through one-off OBA subsidies for access. OBA subsidies are fixed before project implementation but paid only after outputs have been delivered. This mechanism credibly caps available public funding so that service providers are aware that they must bear any cost overruns. Furthermore, the explicit nature of output and subsidy design should clearly identify the risks being taken. In addition, OBA disbursements are usually tied not to the completion of project-input milestones (such as the completion of a telecommunications tower), but rather to delivery of connections (such as pay phones and telecenters) and on meeting specified service delivery targets. The service provider is paid only for the parts of the system that are actually being used. Thus, a disincentive exists for creating excess capacity and a countervailing incentive exists for increasing access. However, to ensure proper incentives for increased access as well as heightened sustainability, tariffs or fees paid by the new customer should cover relevant running costs.

Given the lack of a comprehensive body of literature on benefit shortfalls or cost overruns, or both, in development projects, this chapter compares the results of closed OBA projects with comparable closed World Bank projects. For this review, a sample was analyzed that included all 37 available Implementation Completion Reports for World Bank–funded water, energy, and health projects that closed in fiscal year 2007. This sample was reviewed to identify all projects that have quantifiable outputs as project development objectives.[6]

This sample was compared to 13 completed OBA projects in water, energy, and health for which World Bank Implementation Completion and Results Reports were available.[7] The review shows that 85 percent of OBA projects achieved or overachieved the desired results within or below budget, compared to 49 percent of traditional projects (figure 9.3). Nearly 70 percent of OBA projects were completed below budget, compared to slightly more than half of the traditional projects. Although some of the traditional projects recorded cost overruns, none of the OBA projects did so. Similarly, only two OBA projects (15 percent of the sample) did not achieve the intended results, compared to at least 30 percent of the

Figure 9.3   Comparison of Performance of OBA and Traditional Projects

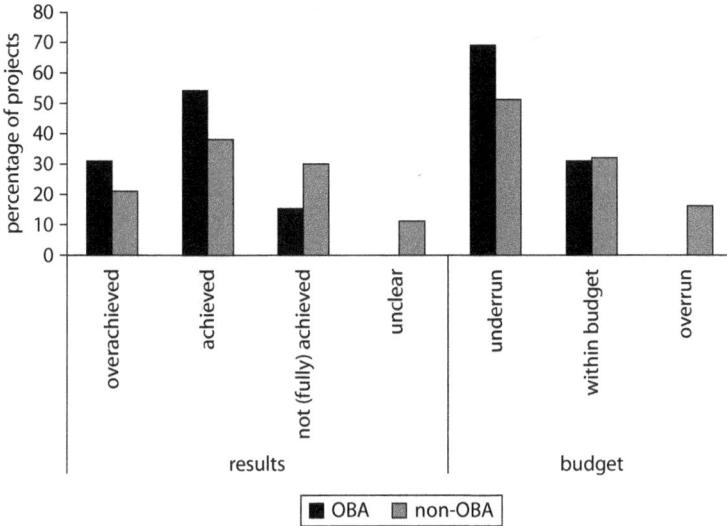

Sources: GPOBA database and World Bank Independent Evaluation Group ratings.

traditional projects reviewed that did not. The two OBA projects that did not deliver all outputs projected disbursed only a small proportion of the funds related to outputs actually delivered.[8] This result provides some indication that OBA can help mitigate risks to the project sponsor of disbursing substantial amounts of funding for projects that do not produce the desired outputs.

Although data are not available for many projects, the results are consistent with the presupposition that OBA shifts performance risk to service providers and helps counteract cost overruns and benefit shortfalls.

Transferring Operational Risk through OBA Subsidies

Are service providers bearing sufficient risk for ongoing service provision after construction is complete? In many public-private partnership (PPP) contracts, whether OBA or not, service providers do bear operational risk. With the addition of an OBA mechanism whereby payments for investments made are actually withheld until preidentified outputs are delivered, OBA schemes can provide an additional hard incentive for performance.

Specific disbursement schedules were obtained for about 64 one-off OBA subsidy projects to estimate the average share of the subsidy that is disbursed upon verification of the different disbursement triggers. The average figures obtained for such projects are respectively: 9% of subsidy disbursed as an advanced payment, 76% of subsidy disbursed upon output delivery, and 15% of subsidy paid upon verification of some service sustained after the output delivery (see figure 9.4).

With ongoing OBA subsidy schemes, particularly those in the health and roads sectors, performance-based payments to service providers are tied to continuous service delivery of a stipulated quality. Performance contracts can define the minimum level of service to be delivered for an agreed payment. This mechanism shifts the performance risk of the project entirely to the service provider, who is to some extent free to decide how to reach performance targets and, therefore, can probably better manage operational risks related to service delivery. As discussed in chapter 4, performance-based road contracts have shifted more ongoing service delivery risk to contractors compared to traditional forced accounts or contracting.

One-off subsidies for access, in contrast, do not necessarily shift performance risk to service providers for the entire duration of their service contracts, unless the project involves significant investment that the service provider must recoup through the tariff. To ensure more sustainable services, OBA projects involving one-off subsidies should take into account the nature of the longer-term service contract and license obligations (see chapter 3 for ICT examples).

Figure 9.4   Transferring Risk When Using One-Off Subsidies

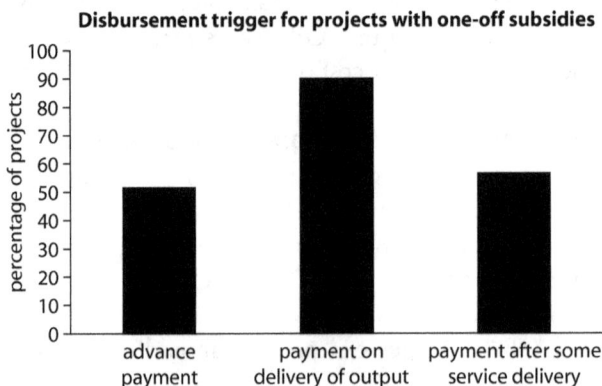

Disbursement trigger for projects with one-off subsidies

Source: GPOBA database.
Note: Figure 9.4 analyzes the 106 projects that use a one-off type of subsidy.

In contrast, the dealer model for off-grid energy solutions has no long-term contracts for service provision. Therefore, the issue of sufficient performance risk transfer—and sustainability—comes into question. To address this issue of long-term sustainability, recent projects involve greater capacity building, product standardization and certification, and even the creation of the medium-term service contract as well as phased subsidy payments, for example, in Bolivia's Decentralized Infrastructure for Rural Transformation project (see chapter 5).

Managing Demand Risk in OBA Schemes

When payments to service providers are made on outputs delivered and those outputs involve the user to apply and make a related down payment, the service provider bears the risk of uptake. Although this risk can be partially mitigated through willingness or ability-to-pay studies and is not completely new to PPP schemes (for example, concession arrangements that involve expansion of services), low uptake is particularly relevant when serving the poor because the poor are often familiar with neither the services (for example, sanitation) nor certain aspects of the services (for example, payment schemes).

Therefore, the demand risk component of OBA schemes can be substantial. It can prolong the time required for project rollout and thus the amount of time required before providers can be reimbursed. Nevertheless, shifting demand risk to the service provider is important, because it helps address the issue of low uptake and because the service provider should manage investments and operations most efficiently to meet required demand:

- Both the Rural Community Water Project in Andhra Pradesh, India (funded by GPOBA), and the Senegal On-Site Sanitation Projects (funded by IDA and GPOBA) use nongovernmental organizations (NGOs) to promote community participation to improve uptake.

- The implementing agency of Colombia's Natural Gas Distribution for Low-Income Families in the Caribbean Coast project reports that natural gas is the first utility service that some of the poorest beneficiaries will receive. Some households were reluctant to access the subsidy, even if the use of gas resulted in a savings compared to traditionally used fuels such as wood and kerosene, because they were reluctant to commit to paying a monthly bill. To mitigate this situation, the implementing agency started outreach campaigns and gave beneficiaries savings boxes to create a habit of saving up for the gas bills. In some cases, distribution companies even initially over-subscribed the program, given the degree of attrition between customer registration and actual service delivery.[9]

Defining the Output

The degree of performance risk shifted to the service provider through OBA schemes depends on the definition of outputs on which subsidies are disbursed. As discussed in chapter 1, traditional procurement of private infrastructure services that contract at the input end of the spectrum, whereby the government may purchase specific inputs or even assets, often does not guarantee that what the government purchases actually will lead to desired outcomes. Therefore, OBA attempts to contract for an output that is as closely related as possible to the desired outcome, while performance risk is still largely under the provider's control.

The definition of outputs has often evolved as OBA has taken root in a sector, and the degree of performance risk that providers are able to bear has in some cases increased. For example, OBA in the ICT sector often used construction or installation milestones as outputs. Over time, outputs have been refined. For example, some of the more effective contracts disburse a portion of subsidies upon installation of the phones and disburse the rest on a regular basis, provided the phones are maintained to standard.

Wide differences can exist from sector to sector and even within projects themselves. The contrast between the small-town component and the greenfield component of the OBA in Water Supply in Uganda's Small Towns and Rural Growth Centers project is set out in more detail in chapter 6 and is an example of such differences. In short, a more pure OBA approach is used where a subproject mainly involves extensions from existing systems, but for the greenfield operations, output-based payments are phased so that 60 percent of the subsidies are disbursed during construction and only 40 percent of the subsidies are disbursed with final connections and water delivery. The difference is attributed to the perception of the private operators' ability to reasonably prefinance the larger construction costs of the greenfield schemes.

Access to Finance and Performance Risk

Effectively shifting performance risk to service providers through OBA requires that service providers are able to prefinance investments and services. This prefinancing can be funded by the service provider through its own cash flow, supplier credit, and other aspects of working capital or by equity and debt financing or by both methods. This financing must be available at a reasonable cost to be affordable for the provider and to minimize the impact of financing costs on the tariff charged to the household. Even in the case of ICT which has moved closer to an ideal OBA model, a portion of OBA subsidies is still often paid up front because of the cost of capital for prefinancing outputs. Another interesting example of how OBA design has attempted to adapt to the access-to-finance constraint is discussed in box 9.2 in relation to the CREMA (Contrato de Recuperación y Mantenimiento) road contracts in Argentina, which were among the first performance-based rehabilitation and maintenance contracts outside the Organisation for Economic Co-operation and Development (OECD).

The access-to-finance constraint seems most binding for sectors or subsectors that rely on small and local or regional providers, as in the off-grid energy schemes, but these constraints may affect the public sector as well. Many public utilities or local municipalities are not in a position to prefinance output delivery. However, exceptions exist. For example, in the Morocco urban water and sanitation pilot (see chapter 6), the public utility of Meknès has taken on commercial debt to prefinance output delivery and allow households to pay their connection costs in installments. Access to finance can become more of an issue for projects that involve contracting out service provision exclusively in a poor area, particularly if the project requires significant investments instead of being able to "leverage" off assets that will also serve wealthier customers (as in the Lesotho Hospital scheme, chapter 7).

To date, limited experience exists on mitigating the access-to-finance constraint with formal financial instruments such as guarantees. One example involves K-Rep Bank in the Kenya water project, which has purchased a partial credit guarantee from the U.S. Agency for International Development's Development (USAID) Credit Authority to reduce the collateral required from borrowers. In many of the countries where OBA is operating, central banks discourage unsecured lending. Thus, banks that prefinance works that will be subsidized with output-based grants still require the borrower to post collateral for the subsidized asset (or portion of the asset), even though OBA is seen as a secure source of funding if performance is met. More work is needed to contract with small and local providers, who are the most likely providers of services in rural and peri-urban areas where access to services is often most needed and access to finance is most constrained.

Box 9.2

CREMA: Phases I and II

Based on positive experience with performance-based road maintenance contracts (see box 4.1 in chapter 4), in 1997 Argentina introduced a new contract combining rehabilitation and maintenance. The Contrato de Recuperación y Mantenimiento (CREMA) requires the contractor to rehabilitate and subsequently maintain a subnetwork of roads for five years for a lump-sum contract. Payments are made when a specified level of service has been achieved. The CREMA contracts implemented between 1997 and 1999 specified that rehabilitation works should be carried out during the first year of the contract. The contractor received 5 to 10 percent of the contract price as an advance payment and additional payments at the end of the first year when rehabilitation works had been completed. The largest percentage of the contract price, however, about 50 percent, was paid in 48 equal monthly installments spread over the remaining four-year contract period. This front-loading of rehabilitation and the delayed payment schedule resulted in contractors financing much of the rehabilitation themselves. The rehabilitation costs sometimes exceeded 50 percent of the contract value.

In the new generation of contracts, Phase II CREMA, the contractor now receives full payment for rehabilitation works executed, proportionate to the outputs achieved during the first 18 months of execution. Although this approach has helped resolve contractors' financing difficulties, it has given rise to another problem. With some contractors receiving up to 80 percent of the contract value for rehabilitation works in the early years of the contract, contractors' incentive to perform their ongoing maintenance obligations across the multiyear life of the contract is reduced. Some contractors have tried to renege on their contracts after they have completed rehabilitation and not fulfill their maintenance obligations.

Nevertheless, the first two phases of Argentina's CREMA program, covering nearly 14,000 kilometers, resulted in significant improvement in the percentage of roads in good condition—from 70 percent in 1998 to 85 percent in 2005. In addition, the percentage of roads in poor condition decreased from 8 percent in 1998 to 4.2 percent in 2005 (World Bank 2006b: 4).

Sources: Cabana, Liautaud, and Faiz 1999; Liautaud 2001; Stankevich, Qureshi, and Queiroz 2005; World Bank 2009e.

Mitigating Payment Risk

Although OBA may shift performance risk to the entity best able to manage that risk, it can also lead to other unintended risks (see box 9.3). One consideration in OBA schemes is payment risk. Even if outputs are

Box 9.3

Limitations on Shifting Risks to Service Providers

Although OBA in general can mitigate the risks of cost overruns and benefit short-falls to governments, donors, or users, as described in this book, one must still take into account factors outside the control of the service provider, as in the case of any well-designed intervention.

- The East Meets West Foundation, an NGO providing output-based connections in the GPOBA-funded Vietnam water scheme, has received an increase in unit subsidy because of unit cost increases partially caused by the recent increase in commodity prices. This situation is especially relevant for projects implemented by small and medium-size service providers who do not have the means to hedge against price increases (this is notably one of the very few examples found where such a unit subsidy adjustment was made).
- In Colombia's Natural Gas Distribution for Low-Income Families in the Caribbean Coast project, the grant agreement specified the unit cost of US$141 to be payable in Colombian pesos. Given the depreciation of the U.S. dollar against the Colombian peso, the actual subsidy payable to the distribution companies was reduced significantly. At the time of the grant agreement signing, the exchange rate was 2,300 Colombian pesos to the U.S. dollar, whereas in 2008, it was only 1,705 pesos to the U.S. dollar. In the Colombian project, the distribution companies effectively absorbed the depreciation.

Following the global financial and economic crisis beginning late 2008, how projects will be affected overall is difficult to predict. By October 2008, the global economic landscape had changed dramatically with the unraveling of the credit markets, yet inflationary pressures have eased considerably because of a crash in commodity and energy prices, with the dollar strengthening against most developing-country currencies. Entities must take these issues into account when structuring an OBA project and have some flexibility to adjust subsidy amounts if the sustainability of the project is at risk.

Sources: GPOBA database and authors.

delivered, what assurance exists that service providers will be paid—and paid on time—even after verification of output delivery? The structure of the flow of funds for an OBA scheme can determine, in the case of competitive schemes, whether the transaction can attract bidders or, in any scheme, whether financial institutions will be comfortable lending to the providers. In the roads sector, CREMA contracts have provided greater assurance to contractors that they will be paid: "By making the long-term payment obligation legally binding on the government, the CREMA has deterred the Treasury from failing to provide funding for road maintenance; and experience during implementation showed that at times of fiscal constraint, the budget process respected the CREMA contracts and funds were allocated to them in priority" (World Bank 2009d).

In some OBA schemes, private fiduciary agents such as banks or well-known multiservice accounting firms have been used to ensure transparent and speedy fund flows. When funds are channeled through the finance ministry or the national (central) banks or both, time, and therefore cost, may increase. One OBA scheme involving a privatized electricity company in Guatemala used the privatization proceeds to fund an OBA facility. The payment risk was guaranteed by breach-of-contract coverage from the Multilateral Investment Guarantee Agency (MIGA), which is part of the WBG.

Private Sector Capital and Expertise

The ratio for leveraging private sector debt and equity in OBA projects with private sector involvement is about 1 to 1.73: for every dollar of subsidy raised, about US$1.73 of private sector financing was mobilized.[10] These estimates refer only to longer-term private investments made and do not include prefinancing in relation to the output-based payments expected in the short and medium-term. For subsidies that partially finance ongoing service provision, the amount of private capital mobilized is difficult to identify. In such projects, the service provider must also prefinance investments for a much longer period. The possibility of mobilizing private finance varies from sector to sector, with ICT and energy mobilizing more than health and water (see sector chapters for more details).

One lesson learned regarding network or utility services is that private finance leveraging is wholly related to tariff reform: ultimately, the service provider must be able to recoup these costs through the tariff. If the aim is to have a smaller amount of subsidy with more of the investment recouped through private financing, the tariff needs to be able to absorb these costs. Frequently, this result will be feasible only if contracts are of a longer nature than is normally accepted. Furthermore, because OBA schemes target the poor, who often are charged social tariffs or who consume small amounts, the possibilities of leveraging in the traditional sense are limited compared to non-OBA schemes that do not target the poor. In any case, user charges should not be set at levels that discourage uptake in sectors with positive externalities, such as health, education, and sanitation.

Another aspect of mobilizing the private sector is encouraging private service providers to connect and serve poor customers whom the private operator would otherwise not serve. OBA schemes that extend existing or newly created assets by providing relatively small amounts of subsidy to incentivize the private operator to reach these poor customers can achieve this goal. For example, previous infrastructure investments may have been made and have excess capacity, but service providers have no real incentive to serve additional, mainly poor customers. OBA interventions in these cases result in very efficient subsidy per capita, whereby relatively small subsidy amounts can connect poor households to a network otherwise unreachable (see box 6.1 on Manila Water and box 9.4 on Colombia Natural Gas). Private sector expertise and discipline brought through OBA schemes can benefit the delivery of social services as well

Box 9.4

Colombia's Natural Gas Project: OBA and the Private Sector

In Colombia, the national regulator sets gas connection prices, and to ensure equity, gas companies are not allowed to offer connection below the regulated price. This situation precludes many of the poorest Colombians from accessing natural gas. In 2006, GPOBA signed a grant agreement with Fundación Promigas, a charitable foundation established by the Colombian gas transportation and distribution company Promigas S.A. The project has connected 35,000 poor households from the lowest two of five socioeconomic strata to the natural gas network.

The subsidized connections were made by regional gas companies owned by Promigas S.A., which marketed the project to the poor target groups, provided payment plans to beneficiaries that allowed them to pay the remaining connection fees over a period of up to five years, and documented connections and consumption of beneficiaries for verification by an independent auditing firm. Subsidies were disbursed only for connections made to households in the two lowest strata who also were provided with a basic stove and who had completed three months of successful billing of services.

The project successfully achieved its target of connecting 35,000 poor households within the estimated time.[a] Promigas S.A. and the gas companies absorbed shortfalls resulting from U.S. dollar depreciations during the project. Fundación Promigas conducted a successful community outreach campaign, creating demand for the subsidized connections. This campaign included measures to convince beneficiaries, for many of whom natural gas is the first utility service that they receive, to commit to paying monthly bills.

a. The gas distribution companies installed 35,000 connections; however, all connections did not meet the criterion of three months of successful billing before the project closed. As a result, disbursements were made for only 34,138 connections.

(for more details on the health and education sectors, see chapters 7 and 8, respectively).

Working with the private sector is not always a panacea for improving access and broader sector reform, and it entails careful consideration and implementation. Capacity can be an issue, especially when working with local authorities and small and local private providers, as seen with off-grid energy or rural water projects, but even in the roads and ICT sectors where OBA is more mainstreamed. Successful projects tend to involve capacity-building elements for the private sector, including learning how to bid for a contract, how much to bid, how to self-monitor against outputs, how to mitigate against payment risk, and so forth.

Key to enhancing private sector finance and expertise will be tackling the constraints of accessing medium- to long-term financing, which would enable greater participation of the private sector not only in OBA but also in PPPs in general (see the "Accountability: Shifting Performance Risk to Providers" section in this chapter for more details). OBA schemes can provide some lessons, especially from the rural energy sector where tackling access to finance seems to have been a priority over the past few years: in poor, off-grid areas, rural affordability increases substantially with microcredit and longer-term fee-for-service arrangements. Typically, 2 to 3 percent of residents can afford cash payment for the service, but with microcredit, the customer base can increase to up to 20 to 30 percent of residents. Longer-term, fee-for-service arrangements could increase the customer base even further (Terrado, Cabraal, and Mukherjee 2008). Chapter 5 describes the role of entities such as Grameen Shakti in Bangladesh's Rural Electrification and Renewable Energy Development project.

Guarantees and other instruments that could work with OBA to leverage financing to provide greater access to the poor for basic services need to be explored further. Guarantees to mitigate risk and increase loan tenure are being used in a Papua New Guinea rural electrification scheme. The program allows credit terms to be extended from three to five years (World Bank 2008b: 132). As OBA schemes grow in scale, World Bank guarantee instruments might play a larger role (for example, partial risk guarantees). Subnational financing instruments will also be critical because many of the basic services discussed here are delegated to or provided at a decentralized level of government.

Innovation and Efficiency

OBA is clearly an innovative mechanism that enables a variety of service solutions to reach the poor. OBA has demonstrated efficiency gains through competition in most sectors when competitive pressures have been applied in the selection of the OBA service provider. Anecdotal evidence, as well as results from a few impact evaluations, shows that the output-based nature of payments has also led to improvements in operational efficiency. Furthermore, the use of output-based arrangements over time in the ICT and roads sectors has possibly led to increased innovation and cost reduction.

Gains from Competition

Using competition to determine the amount of subsidy required is one of the more tested ways to ensure maximum value for money, provided transaction costs do not prove prohibitive and no existing provider is likely to reap significant economies of scale. OBA lends itself readily and transparently to competitive processes, for example through bidding variables like "lowest subsidy required" to meet expected outputs given fixed user charges.[11]

Forty-five projects, mainly in the transport and telecommunications sectors, used competitive bidding to determine service providers (figure 9.5). Competitive selection of service providers is also being used in the water and off-grid energy sectors, as well as in some health projects when NGOs are contracted to provide basic services in a defined area. In some

Figure 9.5   Selection of Service Providers by Method

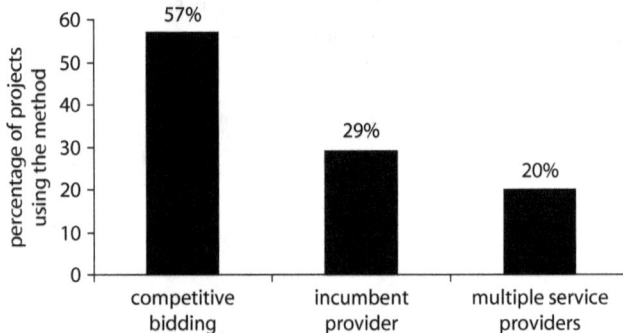

Source: GPOBA database.
Note: The observed universe is 79 projects with some selection method identified. More than one method may be adopted in some projects.

cases, competitive bidding has shown that subprojects were commercially viable and a subsidy was not needed. Another way OBA projects can use competition to increase efficiency is by working with a number of licensed or certified service providers who compete for clients on the basis of quality. This approach is used by 16 projects, in both the health and infrastructure sectors. A sizable proportion of projects (23) work with incumbent service providers, while some projects use other forms of selection (for example, by ranking proposed subprojects based on expected project benefits). A combination of these methods is also possible for some projects.

The following are some examples (see relevant sector chapters for more details) of how OBA projects have resulted in efficiency gains, usually using competitive tendering processes based on lowest subsidy required or greatest numbers of beneficiaries reached:

- In a Mongolian ICT project, competition resulted in 28 percent savings in the total subsidy required for the original areas and beneficiaries to be served. The savings were used to fund the Chulut Soum wireless center, which is estimated to have expanded the project to 1,000 more beneficiaries. In addition, the bidding for the GPOBA-funded OBA scheme expanding mobile phone services in Mongolian towns has demonstrated that mobile phone services can be provided on a commercial basis without subsidies in some cases, although not for Internet services or for facilities such as schools. Many other examples of zero-subsidy bids exist in the ICT sector (for example, in Chile and recently in Nicaragua, where the incumbent offered to pay rather than receive monies from the universal access and service fund to gain market share).

- Bolivia's IDA-funded IDTR (Infraestructura Decentralizada para la Transformación Rural, or Decentralized Infrastructure for Rural Transformation) project for rural electrification led to 25 percent more beneficiaries for the fixed subsidy than the minimum required under the tender and a 40 percent reduction in solar home system (SHS) prices compared with those in a 2004 United Nations Development Programme project in Bolivia.

- In the Sri Lankan rural electrification OBA, one dealer introduced 15 percent price discounting and its own consumer financing, seeking to capture market share.

- Most recently, the competitive bidding process for the OBA in Water Supply in Uganda's Small Towns and Rural Growth Centers project has resulted in an average efficiency gain in 10 towns of about 20 percent, although final results are still to be seen. The bidding also demonstrated that, in some cases, extensions can be made on a commercial basis, with the private sector estimating that it can recoup costs related to new connections through the tariff. Three towns received zero-subsidy bids through competitive tendering.

However, competitive processes take time and can require extensive capacity building, particularly in relation to the tendering process or obtaining access to finance. Furthermore, underbidding during the tender process is a risk, followed by financial problems later, especially if the growth in demand does not materialize as expected. In addition, particularly for small-scale projects, oversophisticated (often donor-led) systems with a wide array of checks and balances may prove costly and cumbersome and lead to inaction. These costs should be weighed against the many obvious advantages of competition to drive down costs through efficiency gains.

For example, lessons from ICT indicate that determining the appropriate level of subsidy often requires projections of demand and necessary investments, which can be complex in dynamic sectors such as ICT and energy. Although large projects may justify this expense, smaller projects may not. In off-grid energy projects, which are perceived as risky and for which technical capacity is often lacking for projects to be undertaken in remote locations, finding bidders can be difficult. In such cases, activities that enhance awareness and capacity building, such as road shows, workshops, business development services, technical training, market surveys, databases on renewable energy resource availability, and institutional building, can all be useful.

Gains from Output-Based Innovation

Other demonstrations of efficiency gains, which may not be as easily quantified, can include quality enhancements or improvement in service delivery. The disbursement of funds *after* service delivery can create strong incentives to deliver outputs in a timely manner.

- For the Armenian Access to Gas and Heat Supply for Poor Urban Households project, evidence shows that timeliness of service delivery and quality of work have led to increased customer satisfaction.
- The provision of telecommunications services to nomadic herder communities in Mongolia required innovative solutions related to difficulties

with determining the adequate size of solar cells and the prediction of beneficiaries' mobility patterns. These difficulties were overcome within the first six months of project operations, and output-based payments most likely helped trigger such a speedy resolution.

- The health sector in postconflict countries (for example, Afghanistan and the Democratic Republic of Congo) has shown that contracting out services to NGOs can lead to quicker and more comprehensive coverage than building up an input-based health system.

The portfolio of OBA schemes analyzed shows a wide array of service providers and a variety of technical solutions. Furthermore, one assumption made at the initiation of OBA was that the focus on outputs would itself enable increased innovation. This expectation has certainly been met in the ICT sector, where service providers have to some extent been free to provide the most appropriate and affordable technology to respond to demand. The general trend in ICT, with or without OBA, is a clear reduction in costs. In addition, however, OBA has brought the recognition that other markets can be tapped and that more pro-poor models of technology, such as prepaid services, can help reach these markets. In the energy sectors, many OBA schemes are bid out as *technology neutral*, although additional subsidies (for example, from the Global Environment Facility) might be provided for renewable energy technologies. In the off-grid Bolivian IDTR project, service providers were required to provide credit to users, but the terms were left up to the service providers. A number of solutions and arrangements (for example, with microfinance institutions) were developed, depending on the technologies, customers, and so forth, which the project team could not have presumed beforehand.

The achievement of cost reduction through OBA relies on the flexibility allowed to service providers to bring their commercial and operational practices into the structuring of OBA schemes. However, the weight of the procurement policies and procedures of governments and donor agencies imposed on the service providers often affects service quality and delivery requirements. These requirements and procedures, rightly aimed at ensuring transparency and competition in the award of publicly funded subsidies, are generally designed for structuring input-based projects. This approach may create bias on how the service providers procure the inputs necessary to deliver the outputs and may limit freedom to proceed as innovatively as service providers would wish. This situation is especially true for smaller service providers and may translate into higher costs. Lessons learned have demonstrated that the key is to specify those essential inputs that cannot be omitted but to leave some degree of discretion beyond that. This flexibility is critical not only in the infrastructure sectors, where long-lived assets should support outputs, but also in the health care sector, where a centralized approach can lead to poor quality that can have a detrimental impact on project outcomes.

The World Bank has begun to address how best to implement output-based approaches within its own operations. A "Guidance Note for Procurement Staff" has been issued (World Bank 2008e; see box 9.5), but more needs to be done, including individualized training. This activity may fit well within the broader push in the Bank to streamline procedures to meet clients' needs more effectively and efficiently, as proposed by the Bank's Operations Policy and Country Services in the recent Concept Note, "Investment Lending Reform." The Concept Note describes the current "disconnect between results focus and inputs-based 'wiring' of [investment loans]" and mentions that the Bank "needs flexible and agile instruments that can easily adapt and respond to changes in the global development business" (World Bank 2009c: 5, 9).

Box 9.5

World Bank Procurement in OBA Projects

A Guidance Note for Procurement Staff, titled "Procurement Issues in Structuring Output-Based Aid (OBA) Operations Financed by the World Bank," was issued April 11, 2008. The note, a joint effort by staff from the GPOBA unit of the Finance, Economics, and Urban Development Department and the Procurement Policy and Services Department, follows up on the November 17, 2005, Guidance Note for Staff, "Structuring Output-Based Aid (OBA) Approaches in World Bank Group Operations," and the Operations Policy and Country Services "Operational Memorandum on the Application of Paragraph 3.13 of the Procurement Guidelines to Cases Involving Incumbent Concessionaires," dated November 7, 2005. It identifies different scenarios and actions required by specialists to facilitate compliance with the Procurement Guidelines in the design of procurement arrangements for the two types of OBA schemes, namely, projects for which there is no existing service provider and projects for which there is already an existing service provider (incumbent concessionaire or equivalent arrangement). The Guidance Note provides illustrative practices and incorporates the lessons learned from procurement assessments conducted under OBA pilot operations across Bank regions.

Source: World Bank 2008e.

Sustainability, Tariffs, and the Enabling Environment

Sustainability of infrastructure and social services schemes implies that an intervention has a long-lasting positive impact rather than short-lived and easily reversible results. Whether OBA schemes have proven to be sustainable on the whole is too early to analyze. No evidence to date suggests that schemes that involve OBA subsidies are less sustainable than their input-based counterparts. Some OBA schemes have been running for many years—in the ICT and roads sectors, in particular. They have been scaled up and replicated elsewhere in their respective regions and even in other regions. To some extent, this endurance is a testament of the sustainability (and, of course, replicability) of the model in these sectors. The evidence on long-term sustainability for off-grid energy projects is limited to a few projects such as the Rural Electrification and Renewable Energy Development projects in Sri Lanka and Bangladesh, which have been operating for over a decade. The results are encouraging. In Sri Lanka, for example, as of June 2008, some 120,000 households were using SHSs, with 750 installations occurring monthly (Terrado, Cabraal, and Mukherjee 2008). The results in Bangladesh are similar; by August 2009, the SHS sales reached 12,500 units per month, with total sales of about 320,000 (GPOBA database). Both projects continue to use grants, but increasingly as methods to reach the poorest segments of the population.

Two characteristics of OBA, in particular, help address the issue of sustainability—the nature of the subsidy design and the performance risk shifted to the providers:

- *Nature of subsidy design.* As previously discussed in detail, OBA schemes are predominantly providing subsidies for access, which are by nature one-off capital subsidies. One-off subsidies do not rely on an ongoing source of subsidy funding. For example, once a household receives the subsidy to connect to a network, a subsidy requirement no longer exists in relation to access for that household.[12]

- *Output-based performance risk.* As discussed in the earlier section of this chapter, "Accountability: Shifting Performance Risk to Providers," by shifting performance risk to service providers, OBA requires service providers to plan and implement schemes to ensure that performance expectations are met if they are to be fully compensated. More careful planning in terms of capacity (given lack of incentives to oversize with OBA) and final output delivery can help enhance sustainability. Furthermore, because demand risk of uptake is largely shifted to service providers, service providers are taking more care in providing appropriate solutions to the targeted customers. The involvement of households and communities in the service expansion process can develop a greater sense of ownership, which in turn enhances sustainability.

Setting of Tariffs and Subsidy Amounts

The sustainability of any OBA scheme—most specifically for network industries—depends on the relationship between the subsidy provided and the tariff charged to consumers for ongoing service provision. For example, where tariffs are lower than running costs, connecting new customers will result in operators incurring losses and having insufficient funds to maintain the system. In such cases, they would have no incentive to serve such customers, thereby rendering service provision unsustainable. Transition tariffs that help raise tariffs to cover running costs could be considered, but the political will to raise tariffs often comes into question, putting the transitional nature of the subsidy at risk. Thus, the scale-up and mainstreaming of OBA in certain sectors such as grid-based water and energy would need to go hand in hand with tariff reform.

Thus, when the poor who are being connected through OBA schemes benefit from subsidized social tariffs, an additional burden can be created on providers who will in turn need to cross-subsidize these new poor users with consumers who are not benefiting from social tariff schemes. This situation has been the experience with connecting the urban poor to the water network in Morocco (see chapter 6) and will likely be the experience with any scheme that connects many new customers benefiting from social tariff schemes.

However, it is important to differentiate between costs that are covered by the tariff regime and those that are not. At the given tariff levels (including regulated connection charges), the tariff as a whole may be set to ensure that the utility recovers sufficient costs of serving its entire jurisdiction, including the low-income area under consideration for an OBA scheme. Furthermore, the utility may already have made certain performance promises to the regulator (for example, connecting low-income communities) as part of the last tariff review, so the OBA design must take account of such possible regulatory obligations of the utility.

These issues were encountered in the case of the OBA design for an electricity scheme for slum areas of Mumbai, India (see chapter 5). The distribution company is obligated to provide a metered working connection to anyone who applies. The regulated connection charge covers these costs (and upstream costs of providing the connection). The costs of connections from the meter to the house and of internal wiring are not addressed by the utility or the regulator and need to be faced fully by the slum dweller and, thus, are creating the bottleneck to uptake. After a subsidy is provided here, the distribution company has the incentive to carry out upstream investment without any need for subsidy support (because the tariff regime compensates for this investment).

Furthermore, in the case of a multiyear tariff regime set by the regulator, the utility may be in a position to earn extra returns from reducing technical and commercial losses (because the tariffs are set for the multiyear regulatory period and include the cost of losses). In that case, connections for low-income consumers that help reduce theft—and therefore reduce commercial losses—may increase returns to the utility. The utility may therefore have adequate commercial incentive (and returns) to undertake a certain amount of connection activity in low-income areas without subsidy support. To design more economical and politically sustainable solutions, OBA schemes need to balance these factors to ensure an appropriate level of subsidies that incentivizes the provider but does not overcompensate it.

Sustainability

The sustainability of the funding source needs to be considered in relation to the subsidy design mechanism. For example, in the case of roads and health schemes that rely on ongoing subsidy streams, the sustainability of any given scheme depends on a constant flow of subsidies. Road maintenance funds in developed countries may provide a certain degree of security and sustainability, but road maintenance funds in developing countries have a more mixed record. The health sector often does not have that type of earmarked subsidy pool and, therefore, relies mainly on the budget made available by the government. This situation makes ring-fencing the health budget allocated to performance-based schemes more difficult, although such a risk also applies to traditional methods of providing health care.

The ICT sector seems to have a more robust form of subsidy funding. In ICT, levies, auctions, and government budgets collected into universal access and service funds (UASF) have been reliable in providing the required funding. Levies on telecommunications operators' revenues may be preferable because they may be seen as more reliable and sustainable from a private sector perspective, in contrast to government budget funding or spectrum auctions. However, although the funding source has generally been reliable in ICT, the political sustainability of the approach has been problematic because of large sums being accumulated but not being disbursed in a timely manner (see chapter 3).

Moreover, a scheme is only sustainable in terms of the subsidy required if the subsidy amounts are reasonable and reflect the appropriate cost and benefit. Efficiency gains through innovation and competition therefore contribute to sustainability. Nevertheless, subsidy per capita can vary significantly between regions and sectors, depending on the scope of service to be subsidized. Connecting the poor to grid-based infrastructure services can be relatively cheap where trunk infrastructure exists and only the connection itself needs to be subsidized. The same service in a similar geographic area can require much higher subsidies if distribution and production infrastructure needs to be subsidized.

For example, the subsidy for natural gas connections (including a gas heater) in Armenia is US$160.00, whereas the connection subsidy to the electricity grid in densely populated rural Ethiopia, with its relatively larger families, is US$6.25. Those figures compare to US$115.00 per capita for the installation of an SHS in very remote areas of rural Bolivia. Similarly, per capita subsidies for water projects range from US$125.00 in Morocco, where subsidies include sanitation connections, to US$6.20 in Kampala, Uganda, in a project that makes extensive use of public water points and shared yard taps. Those numbers, although different because of different project contexts, have all shown sufficient economic rates of return in cases where information on economic rates of return was analyzed for this book (where funding is by GPOBA).

Enabling Environment

An OBA scheme is only as sustainable as the environment in which it operates. Because pilots are often short-term interventions, they may seem to be isolated from broader sector reform issues in the short term. But for greater impact with scaling-up and mainstreaming, a supportive enabling environment is critical. The following aspects of an enabling environment—most of which are interrelated and many of which are common requirements for successful PPP in the sector—seem to play a particularly important role in the success of OBA in any given region or sector:

- Market structure and experience with competitive processes to encourage efficiency
- Regulatory framework or legal or contractual framework for the sector, including tariff-setting and adjustment policies
- Capacity of implementing agencies, for example, to handle procurement and transaction processes, monitoring and verification, and funds flow, and also in relation to understanding of and willingness to work with performance-based arrangements
- Extent of experience with the private sector in service provision, where relevant.

For example, output-based grid and minigrid projects cannot bypass the need for a strong regulatory regime or at least robust contractual (and supporting legal) arrangements. This need could partially explain the limited use of OBA in grid and minigrid projects because many of the developing countries have weak regulatory capacity to enforce or oversee provider performance and the costs of regulation in remote areas are very high (Reiche, Rysankova, and Goldmark 2006: 46). At the same time, a light-handed approach to regulation may be required with respect to service standards: to provide services that the poor can afford and to more effectively use self-selection targeting methods, for example, service standards may sometimes need to be relaxed—although always meeting a minimum standard (Baker and Tremolet 2000).

The importance of an appropriate legal and regulatory environment is also demonstrated through the previous discussion of tariff and regulation. Without proper regulatory accounting (or, at the minimum, a capacity to understand the issues at hand), tariff and subsidy policies could lead to misalignment of incentives or waste of limited resources or both. Less optimal and sustainable solutions are likely to result.

Monitoring of Results in Traditional World Bank Projects

The *2009 Annual Review of Development Effectiveness* by the World Bank's Independent Evaluation Group highlights results monitoring as an area of concern in World Bank projects. Independent Evaluation Group ratings of monitoring and evaluation (M&E) systems "from projects closing in fiscal 2007 and 2008 show that only 37 percent of projects exiting the portfolio received ratings of high or substantial, while the remaining 63 percent were rated modest or negligible" (World Bank 2009a: p.26f). One possible explanation suggested in the report is that the project approval process does not sufficiently focus on results monitoring, so staff are not rewarded for implementing good M&E systems. The report states that "if M&E is seen as a secondary issue, simply a tax on overburdened Bank staff, mandates and requirements are unlikely to result in the collection and use of more meaningful information" (World Bank 2009a: p.27). Issues cited are indicators that are not clearly defined or not measurable. At the same time, the review shows a clear correlation between the quality of M&E systems and overall project outcomes.

The main reasons identified for the poor performance of M&E systems of many projects are a lack of staff incentives to focus on M&E and a "culture of approval" resulting from a "drive to get projects launched" (World Bank 2009a: p27). OBA schemes can help mitigate this situation because they require output verification prior to disbursement of subsidies, which helps internalize monitoring, making it a key design element essential to the project design process. However, the degree and quality of monitoring and verification vary from scheme to scheme, more than from sector to sector. The effectiveness of monitoring is related to several factors:

- *The definition of the output to be monitored.* The ease of measuring and verifying the delivery of the output is closely related to how it is defined.
- *The availability of trained local consultants and engineers to effectively monitor the delivery of outputs.* Capacity is a greater issue when the outputs to be verified are more complicated.
- *The chance of capture of monitoring agents by service providers.* Capture is greater when the verification agent is smaller and the service provider is more powerful. In some cases, projects may have to look outside of the country for a viable verification agent.
- *The capacity of the local government institutions to accept and interpret the monitoring results and to use the results for intended purposes.* Even

if the verification agent does his or her job correctly and on time, is the government (if involved) able and appropriately incentivized to quickly and effectively process that information for timely subsidy disbursement?

Whether an OBA scheme will result in the appropriate output and disbursement information being provided for broader M&E purposes depends on the recording and information dissemination process. In World Bank OBA projects, this process is dependent on the feedback loop between the governments or project implementation units on the ground and their relevant Bank task teams, who in turn would need to systematically record the data where they could be shared and evaluated. The experience through this review demonstrated that although GPOBA-funded projects required an output-oriented monitoring and information-sharing system, many Bank-funded OBA projects did not involve such a feedback loop, sometimes because the OBA component of a Bank-funded project was only a small component of a much larger input-based program. Output-oriented monitoring in the World Bank is expected to improve with the adoption of core indicators for each sector (and subsector). Core indicators for the sectors approved so far are consistent with indicators monitored in OBA projects.

Best practice would use the monitoring platform of OBA beyond the verification of outputs to check how outcomes and other aspects of service delivery are faring. However, this process is often the weakest link in the feedback loop between OBA planning, design, and implementation. Although OBA internalizes the monitoring of outputs, the monitoring framework established is rarely used for purposes other than payment of subsidies; hence, the benefit of the information collected (for example, to improve quality of service) is not always exploited in full. Alternatively, in some cases, additional information is not collected for long-term gain because of short-term costs. All sectors may be able to draw lessons from some performance-based roads schemes that are attempting to enable even users to report and monitor performance by making performance criteria easily measurable or discernible. Impact evaluations are a good way to supplement verification activities. Furthermore, impact evaluations comparing output-based and input-based approaches should be considered; a few such impact evaluations are being attempted.

These enhancements to monitoring and verification under OBA schemes require capacity and resources. Verification agents must be appropriately trained as well as incentivized. GPOBA uses for the most part third-party verification agents to help enhance transparency and improve effectiveness so that outputs can be verified relatively quickly and the much needed disbursements can be made. The key is to balance the independence of output verification with the broader sector-monitoring needs and to ensure ownership on the part of the regulatory or relevant government agency. A recent case of overreporting of outputs achieved and the resulting excess performance payments made under performance contracts between the Global Alliance for Vaccines and Immunization and several recipient countries provides an example of how, without proper monitoring, the advantages of results-based schemes can be called into serious question.

Monitoring for improved governance. With OBA schemes, accountability also increases for donors and governments: public funding is linked to the delivery of preidentified outputs, and, therefore, waste or inappropriate allocation should be minimized. Thus, OBA can play an important role in the fight to improve governance and reduce corruption. OBA projects should make full use of the requirement to monitor for outputs, through physical audit, surveys of beneficiaries, and oversight by civil society. For support of broad monitoring, OBA projects should include an active communication strategy that advertises what services are to be delivered to whom and at what price, as is currently being done in Morocco's urban water sector (chapter 6). However, although project-specific outputs may be easy to monitor, compliance with general regulations or laws governing the sector may be less transparent. Detecting poor construction or below-standard delivery can be difficult, and therefore outputs should be defined appropriately; bidding documents specified carefully; and existing laws and standards enforced through regulation, contract monitoring, or both, demonstrating the importance, once again, of how an enabling environment can shape the success of an OBA scheme (Mumssen and Kenny, 2007).

Notes

1. The GPOBA monitoring and evaluation team has also explored the option of using unit cost data from the World Bank Africa Infrastructure Country Diagnostic Study. However, the study uses a more disaggregated concept of unit costs that does not allow a systematic comparison. The study includes outputs such as the meters of pipe of a certain quality and diameter laid or of standposts installed, whereas the unit cost definitions for OBA can include necessary network extension and installation of final connections.

2. Quantity-based subsidies through tariffs in ICT are less common because the sector has moved toward collecting explicit subsidies through universal access funds, but such subsidies are still in place in some former Soviet bloc countries.

3. Well-designed OBA schemes in the utility sectors usually rely on a target population that can afford sustainable tariffs that cover ongoing costs of service provision. That is, although access may be subsidized, tariffs or the running or operating costs may not be. These costs are often not a major hurdle: the poor usually are paying more for alternative services (UNDP 2006: 52, 83). In some cases, additional pro-poor mechanisms are required to ensure effective targeting. For example, tariff affordability issues for the very poorest households can be partially mitigated by subsidizing pro-poor access mechanisms (such as public water points), which have lower running costs per capita, and by ensuring appropriate schemes that fit the payment patterns of the poor. On the basis of extensive research on the patterns of service delivery to and consumption by the poor, one can conclude that the poor are on the whole paying more per unit of service consumed, and are often receiving inferior quality. This finding indicates that tariffs that cover the ongoing cost of service delivery are likely not a major hurdle for the poor (Bardasi and Wodon 2008).

4. Of the remaining projects, most are transport projects that finance road infrastructure accessible to the general public, and therefore a specific targeting methodology does not apply.

5. Enhanced accountability in the use of public funds and potential reduction in corruption are discussed in the section of this chapter titled "Monitoring of Results."

6. Projects with project development objectives relating to policy formulation or institutional strengthening, or both, or consisting of project development objectives with higher-level project impacts not exclusively under the control of the project implementer were excluded from the analysis because of the inability to compare them to OBA.

7. The analysis uses information from Implementation Completion Reports for projects funded by the IDA and the IBRD and information from the Global

Environment Facility Web site for projects funded by it. A number of projects closed shortly before this review, therefore ICR's are not available.

8. Funds disbursed included some fixed costs related to setting up the project.

9. Colombia Natural Gas Project, Implementation Completion and Results Report, April 2009.

10. The ratio is derived from 33 private sector projects for which the amount of private financing could be identified. This ratio is not based on the whole sample of OBA projects identified because of (a) lack of data availability, (b) ongoing subsidies for which private financing may be leveraged but is very difficult to quantify, and (c) projects that do not involve the private sector.

11. On the basis of reviewed experience, including from the Paraguay water OBA that attempted both forms of bidding, this book recommends fixing tariff levels ex ante and bidding on the minimum subsidy per connection (or maximum beneficiaries served, given a set subsidy). This approach would prevent any resentment from the regulator or users about inequity of tariffs across the country and would also allow inclusion of a lifeline tariff if the national policy requires one.

12. However, for enhancement of the sustainability of services, one-off OBA schemes may withhold a portion of the subsidy disbursement after, for example, several months of bills paid or collected or both. In addition, this approach assumes that the household can afford ongoing operations and maintenance costs (for example, in the form of tariffs). On the whole, this factor is not a major hurdle. (see Note 3 above)

## CHAPTER 10

Key Considerations for Moving Forward

The piloting phase of output-based aid (OBA) has generally been a success. About 131 OBA projects have been implemented or are under way in the World Bank Group (WBG). At a minimum, these projects are expected to reach almost 61 million beneficiaries worldwide.[1] The pilots in the Chilean information and communication technology (ICT) sector and the Argentine roads sector in the 1990s led to scale-up in their respective countries and eventual replication worldwide. One can now safely say that OBA approaches have become mainstreamed as one of the key modus operandi for interventions in these two sectors in many parts of the world. In the health and off-grid energy sectors, OBA approaches are recognized as one of the key financing mechanisms to expand targeted access to the poor and is widely used. In the water, education, and grid-based energy sectors, OBA is still in the pilot stage.

Although OBA is increasingly used as a tool to increase access to basic services, the percentage of the OBA portfolio compared to overall activities by the International Bank for Reconstruction and Development (IBRD) and the International Development Association (IDA) is small. About 2.7 percent of the World Bank project portfolio in the transport, ICT, health, water and sanitation, energy, and education sectors approved between fiscal years 2000 and 2009 used an OBA approach.[2] The ICT sector used OBA most commonly,[3] with 9.1 percent of its portfolio using OBA, followed by health (7.1 percent) and transport (3.6 percent). Thus, although OBA is gaining ground and recognition, scaling-up is still needed to make real strides toward improving access to basic services for the poor.

OBA's prevalence in some sectors, and its origination in Latin America in the 1990s, is largely related to sector and country circumstances. More specifically, for an OBA approach to be viable, service providers must be able to take on performance risk and, in particular, prefinance investments until subsidies are disbursed on the basis of output verification. Although several cases exist of OBA with public sector providers, private sector operators traditionally are better structured to respond to performance-based incentives[4] and are usually better able to prefinance outputs. Thus, a correlation appears to exist between the prevalence of OBA and the sector and regional experience with public-private partnerships. This finding would imply that OBA will take stronger root where contractual and regulatory practices traditionally have been more supportive of the private sector taking risks. At the same time, OBA can be an important mechanism through which efficiency gains from sector reform are shared with users through improved access and can thereby help underscore the benefits of public-private partnerships where appropriate.

The lessons learned regarding the use of OBA compared to traditional approaches to contracting have demonstrated that *OBA can be used to help more efficiently target subsidies and mobilize the private sector to serve poor households* that would otherwise go without improved service. OBA has also demonstrated that *monitoring for results is possible* if appropriate systems for capturing and transmitting results are put in place. At the same time, this book recognizes that *OBA is not a substitute for sector reform.* The experience of government contracting with the private sector and, to some extent, the existence of legal or regulatory practices that are more supportive of private sector risk taking, are part of the environment that enables OBA to be more successful in some contexts than in others. In turn, OBA is one of the mechanisms through which efficiency gains from sector reform have been shared with users through improved access and improved standards of service. *Therefore, OBA not only relies on a supportive enabling environment but also can itself help underscore the benefits.*

Cross-cutting challenges for successful OBA schemes remain, even for those sectors where OBA is already more mainstreamed as one of the principal ways to expand access to services. Although some of these challenges apply to input-based approaches as well, they must be addressed for OBA to continue to have an impact.

- *Access to finance.* Access to finance can be a hurdle for OBA schemes in all sectors, even in ICT. The current financial crisis is likely to exacerbate this problem. Access to finance can present a hurdle for both providers and users, resulting in the following challenges: (a) difficulty in shifting sufficient performance risk to service providers under an OBA arrangement if the cost of prefinancing the outputs would place an undue burden on the provider or if the resulting fees to users (for example, tariffs) would be unaffordable, or both; and (b) limitations on developing a vibrant private sector that can afford to take risks and invest in business expansion, even with the availability of targeted subsidies to help defray the costs. In a few cases, guarantees and lines of credit to the banking sector are being tested. Where such financing instruments are not as readily available, OBA schemes may need to phase in payments against reasonable milestones, provided performance risk for output delivery remains largely with the service provider.

- *Security and sustainability of funding.* A secure source of funding and an administrative framework that allow swift disbursement when outputs have been achieved are required. Furthermore, for the sustainability of OBA in any given sector, the source of funding needs to be reliable and consistent. Lessons are being learned—regarding both benefits and challenges—from existing arrangements being used in the ICT, roads, and energy sectors (for example, from universal access and service funds in ICT).

- *Capacity.* Capacity to implement and monitor OBA schemes can be limited, particularly in those countries and sectors where increased access is most urgently needed. These capacity limitations are often related to transaction design and implementation, output monitoring and verification, and demand management. Targeted training, hiring of independent verification agents, involvement of nongovernmental organizations, and use of private administrators to manage universal access funds are all part of more successful solutions being implemented to mitigate capacity constraints.

- *Enabling environment.* For OBA schemes to be sustainable and increase in scale, some basic institutions and processes that support the development, monitoring, and adjustment of contracts should be in place. Sufficiently transparent legal or regulatory arrangements (for example, for tariff setting and adjustment—which are critical in the determination of appropriate subsidy levels) would be among such enabling factors and would ultimately aim to reduce perceived risk to providers and, to some extent, the cost to final users.

- *Internal environment.* For governments, donor agencies, and multilateral institutions to mainstream OBA approaches, careful consideration and, in many cases, new rules or procedures are needed that allow output-based disbursement and procurement systems that do not focus largely on inputs. Such changes would provide project managers with more incentives to work more confidently with innovative approaches such as OBA. For example, the Bank is currently considering reforms to its investment lending products which could allow wider and more effective use of results-based financing instruments.

- *Targeting.* As the size of pilots and programs increases, and as technologies change, more refined targeting mechanisms will be required. These can be costly to administer and require additional capacity, but such costs may outweigh the leakage from large geographically targeted schemes. A blend of targeting mechanisms is proving effective.

- *Donor coordination.* Ultimately, all else being equal, service providers will opt for input-based schemes because they transfer less risk to the provider. However, donors and governments should be looking to transfer more risk to providers to hold them accountable (as long as providers are equipped to take on that risk). If OBA is to be the mechanism chosen for a given intervention, donor or government coordination is required.

Based on the experiences so far, a good case exists for mainstreaming OBA as a tool to improve pro-poor access to basic services. Developing countries could work with the international donor community to adopt OBA more widely in sectors where experience on how to scale up OBA approaches is already available and to further pilot OBA in sectors that show promise. The advantages of OBA discussed in this book make OBA a good tool for use as part of a country-based development model. OBA can help donors to align around country-driven goals. Whereas donor activities often focus on traditional project aid that uses complex centralized systems to finance inputs, OBA focuses on funding based on results. Pooling donor funds to pay for results delegates the coordination to qualified service providers with a financial incentive to find efficient solutions to reach those goals. OBA provides a mechanism of mutual accountability that can promote the goal of the country-based development model of ensuring "that both national governments and donors are responsible for meeting their commitments to country-based development" (World Bank 2007a: 1). OBA can also assist in the definition of outputs and outcomes in results-based country assistance strategies, especially in IDA countries that need to strengthen their results focus.

The Bank could support the wider donor community by transferring lessons from OBA and related sector reform from country to country and between sectors (for example, between universal access and service funds in ICT, road maintenance funds, and rural electrification funds). This will help OBA practitioners across sectors and regions benefit from the lessons learned over the past decade, while tailoring such lessons to specific contexts. The Bank should also continue its important work on regulatory reform (for example, through the newly created Regulatory Thematic Group) and on promotion of the agenda for sustainable tariffs and subsidy policies that are pro-poor. In some cases, OBA can help provide the starting point for these policy discussions to help improve the efficiency of scarce public resources while increasing access to basic services to the poor through, for example, public-private partnerships.

Greater WBG coordination is also key to successful scale-up of such results-based approaches. The Bank and the International Finance (IFC) Corporation could work together to provide financial solutions to mitigate the access-to-finance constraint by encouraging banks to improve lending conditions to service providers both for prefinancing of outputs and for longer-term project finance. Also, capacity building and technical assistance (for example, for transaction support, tariff design and subsidy policy, and monitoring and evaluation) can be provided by the WBG and multidonor programs such as PPIAF (Public-Private Infrastructure Advisory Facility), ESMAP (Energy Sector Management Assistance Program), WSP (Water and Sanitation Program), and GPOBA (Global Partnership on Output-Based Aid).

GPOBA is stepping up its efforts to facilitate sharing of experiences and best practices in OBA, and to provide WBG staff and other development partners with the practical knowledge they need to assess when OBA is suitable and to design and implement OBA schemes. This approach is in line with GPOBA's strategy to evolve within the coming three to five years from providing subsidy funding to acting primarily as a center of OBA expertise. The latter includes activities such as holding training events, developing online resources and an e-learning course, and developing a diagnostic tool that would provide more guidance to development practitioners on issues such as project design and relevant characteristics of an enabling environment for OBA schemes.

However, the ultimate decision on the success of OBA or any other aid effectiveness tool to improve access to the poor and enhance accountability rests with the developing country governments, and their interest, ownership, and commitment to design and sustain such approaches. The donor community needs to ensure it speaks with one common voice on the issues related to transparency and efficient use of resources to reach the poorest. The WBG has a central role to play in demonstrating that OBA, a key part of the results-based financing approach, can help improve access to basic services and reach the Millennium Development Goals. The existing information and expertise on OBA, including this book, provide a solid underpinning for the successful design of pilots or programs that respond to client needs.

Notes

1. Data on the number of beneficiaries are not readily available for public access, namely some information and communication technology and transport projects. Beneficiary information is particularly limited in the roads sector (available only in 2 of the 23 World Bank–implemented projects) because of the nonexclusivity of roads projects.

2. Several factors have contributed to this low percentage, aside from OBA not being fully mainstreamed. Although the WBG OBA portfolio only includes projects that aim at increasing household access to basic services, the overall WBG portfolio also includes projects financing large upstream investments, wider sector-reform programs, analytic and advisory activities, and so forth. In addition, the overall WBG portfolio obtained from the WBG Business Warehouse includes subsectors such as mining, railways, ports, and nutrition for which no OBA projects have been identified.

3. However, between fiscal years 2000 and 2009, the overall ICT portfolio is relatively small (US$807 million), compared to transport (over US$31 billion), which helps explain the small absolute value of OBA subsidies in ICT even though OBA is mainstreamed more in that sector than in any other.

OBA subsidies in the ICT sector mainly were financed through levies on service providers and not through donor funds, so that the exact subsidy amounts depend on service provider revenues and are unknown at the start of the project. The review identified at least US$6.2 billion in levies that were used to fund universal access funds.

4. Because of ownership change from public to private, increases in labor productivity, service quality, and investment have been reported in competitive markets. For more sources on gains in productivity and profitability associated with privatization, see Gassner, Popov, and Pushak (2007: 3 n6).

Output-Based Aid Projects in the World Bank Group, March 30, 2009

Telecommunications

Project name (PO number)	Country or region	Funding source	Type of output	World Bank subsidy amount including GPOBA[a] (US$)	Planned number of beneficiaries	Project status (latest information on actual number of beneficiaries[b])
1 OBA Telecommunications (P081250)	Azerbaijan (ECA)	TBC[?]	TBC	TBC	TBC	Design
2 Competitiveness and Enterprise Development (P071443)	Burkina Faso (AFR)	IDA	Pay phones and PoPs	1,039,724	485,146	Implementation
3 Rural Telecommunication Access (P102475)	Cambodia (EAP)	GPOBA	Beneficiaries	2,500,957	261,000	Implementation
4 Infrastructure for Territorial Development (P076807)	Chile (LAC)	TBC	Public phones	TBC	TBC	Implementation
5 Power and Communications Sectors Modernization and Rural Services (P063644)	Ecuador (LAC)	IBRD	Pay phones and Internet stations	4,150,000	TBC	Closed (0)[c]
6 OBA and Regulatory Frameworks for Rural and Peri-Urban Telecommunications (P094321)	Guatemala (LAC)	IBRD	Public phones	16,000,000	3,500,000	Implementation
7 Rural Telecommunications Development (P093925)	India (SAR)	IDA	Public phones and Internet	TBC	TBC	Design
8 Extending Telecommunications in Rural Indonesia (P102476)	Indonesia (EAP)	GPOBA	Direct users	1,868,338	758,250	Implementation

#	Project	Country (region)	Financing	Service			Status
9	Rural Infrastructure Services (P057761)	Malawi (AFR)	IDA	Pay phones, telecenters, and Internet stations	1,500,000	TBC	Implementation
10	OBA Pilot Project of Universal Access Strategy (P102488)	Mongolia (EAP)	GPOBA	Pay phones, telecenters, and Internet stations	257,335	21,312	Closed (22,315)[d]
11	Information and Communications Infrastructure Development (P092965)	Mongolia (EAP)	IDA	Pay phones, telecenters, and Internet stations	5,450,000	45,000	Implementation
12	Mozambique Communication Sector Reform (P073479)	Mozambique (AFR)	IDA	Pay phones and Internet PoPs	3,000,000	2,600,000	Closed
13	Telecommunications Sector Reform (P050671)	Nepal (SAR)	IDA	Access lines	11,900,000	4,000,000	Closed
14	Telecommunications Reform (P055853)	Nicaragua (LAC)	IDA	Pay phones	900,000	323,000	Closed
15	Rural Telecommunications (P089989)	Nicaragua (LAC)	IDA	Pay phones and Internet PoPs	7,900,000	376,000	Implementation
16	Privatization Support (ICT) (P070293)	Nigeria (AFR)	IDA	Pay phones and Internet stations	6,130,000	1,683,422	Implementation
17	Telecommunications and Postal Sector Reform (P075739)	Samoa (EAP)	TBC	Pay phones and Internet stations	TBC	TBC	Implementation
18	Telecommunications and ICT Development (P088448)	St. Lucia (LAC)	IDA, IBRD	Access lines and Internet	1,000,000	TBC	Implementation
19	Energy for Rural Transformation (P069996)	Uganda (AFR)	IDA	Internet POPs and public phones	6,695,981	3,600,000	Closed
20	Increased Access to Electricity and ICT Services (P077452)	Zambia (AFR)	IDA	Public phones, PoPs, access center, and IXP	3,125,000	TBC	Implementation

(continued)

Project name (PO number)	Country or region	Funding source	Type of output	World Bank subsidy amount including GPOBA[a] (US$)	Planned number of beneficiaries	Project status (latest information on actual number of beneficiaries[b])
Transport						
1 Road Maintenance and Sector Rehabilitation (P006003)	Argentina (LAC)	IBRD	11,667 km	248,300,000	n.a.[k]	Closed
2 National Highway Asset Management (P088153)	Argentina (LCR)	IBRD	8,188 km	182,800,000	n.a.	Implementation
3 Provincial Road Infrastructure (P070628)	Argentina (LCR)	IBRD	2,204 km	96,400,000	n.a.	Implementation
4 National Highway Rehabilitation and Maintenance (P052590)	Argentina (LAC)	IBRD, national government	19,885 km	295,775,000	n.a.	Closed
5 Federal Highways (P006532)	Brazil (LAC)	IBRD, national government	3,500 km[e]	247,700,000	n.a.	Closed
6 Rio Grande do Sul Highway Management (P034578)	Brazil (LAC)	IBRD, national government	2,200 km	70,000,000	n.a.	Closed
7 Transport Sector (P074030)	Burkina Faso (AFR)	IDA	1,021 km	TBC	n.a.	Implementation
8 OBA in Road Network Management and Maintenance 2 (P087004)	Cape Verde (AFR)	IDA	225 km	6,900,000	n.a.	Implementation
9 National Transport Program Support (P035672)	Chad (AFR)	IDA	440 km	11,088,000	n.a.	Closed
10 Road Network Management and Maintenance (P079736)	Chad (AFR)	IDA, national government	600 km	24,000,000	n.a.	Implementation
11 India—Annuity Road Projects (TBC)	India (SAR)	TBC	TBC	TBC	n.a.	Implementation

#	Project	Country (region)	Funding source				Status
12	Northern Corridor Transport Improvement (P082615)	Kenya (AFR)	IDA, NDF, national government	300 km	207,000,000	n.a.	Implementation
13	Transport Infrastructure Investment (P082806)	Madagascar (AFR)	IDA	TBC	27,600,000	n.a.	Implementation
14	Nigeria Federal Roads Development (P090135)	Nigeria (AFR)	IDA, national government	1,800 km	330,000,000	n.a.	Implementation
15	Road Maintenance (P082026)	Paraguay (LAC)	IBRD	968 km	39,270,000	n.a.	Implementation
16	Transport Project II (P049267)	Uruguay (LAC)	IBRD, national government	856 km	42,237,000	n.a.	Closed
17	Second Rural Access (P085231)	Yemen (MENA)	IDA, national government	950 km	40,000,000	250,000	Implementation
18	Transport Sector Support Program (P055120)	Tanzania (AFR)	IDA	708 km	3,000,000	TBC	Design
19	Road Network Management and Maintenance (P088645, GPOBA); (P078387, World Bank)	Tanzania (AFR)	IDA	850 km	26,000,000	TBC	Implementation
20	Regional Transport Infrastructure Decentralization (Provias Descentralizado) (P078813)	Peru (LAC)	IBRD IADB, national government	4,906 km	50,000,000	TBC	Implementation
21	Second Rural Roads (P044601)	Peru (LAC)	IBRD, IADB, national government	14,950 km	23,154,000	3,500,000	Closed (3,500,000)
22	Rural Road Rehabilitation and Maintenance (P037047)	Peru (LAC)	IBRD, IADB, national government	10,881 km	7,390,000	1,500,000	Closed (3,500,000)
23	Transport Rehabilitation (P075207)	Serbia and Montenegro (ECA)	IDA, national government	1,200 km	55,000,000	TBC	Implementation

(continued)

Energy

Project name (PO number)	Country or region	Funding source	Type of output	World Bank subsidy amount including GPOBA[a] (US$)	Planned number of beneficiaries	Project status (latest information on actual number of beneficiaries[b])
1 Renewable Energy in the Rural Market (P006043)	Argentina (LAC)	IBRD	Household connections	30,600,000	180,000	Implementation (48,000)
2 Access to Gas and Heat Supply for Poor Urban Households (P103071)	Armenia (ECA)	GPOBA	Individual gas connections	3,100,000	18,676	Implementation (11,470)
3 Heating and Gas (IDA Project) (P095329)	Armenia (ECA)	IDA, national government	Individual gas connections	3,000,000	21,924	Implementation (8,300)
4 Rural Electrification and Renewable Energy Development (IDCOL SHS) (P071794)	Bangladesh (SAR)	GEF, IDA, ADB, IDB, KfW, GTZ	SHS installations	8,200,000	1,221,960	Implementation (1,800,000)
5 Bangladesh Rural Electrification and Renewable Energy—Phase II (SHS) (P119549)	Bangladesh (SAR)	GPOBA, IDA, ADB, IDB, KfW, GTZ	SHS installations	7,000,000	840,000	Design
6 Bangladesh Rural Electrification and Renewable Energy—Phase II (mini-grids) (P119547)	Bangladesh (SAR)	GPOBA, IDA, ADB, JICA, KfW	Household connection to the mini-grids	1,000,000	22,500	Design
7 Decentralized Infrastructure for Rural Transformation (P073367)	Bolivia (LAC)	IDA	SHS installations	10,000,000	106,746	Implementation (30,776)
8 Bolivia Decentralized Electricity for Universal Access (P102479)	Bolivia (LAC)	GPOBA	SHS and pico-PV systems	5,175,000	45,000	Implementation

#	Project	Country (Region)	Funding	Unit			Status
9	Rural Electrification and Transmission (P071591, P064844)	Cambodia (EAP)	GEF	Household connections	5,600,000	316,200	Implementation
10	Renewable Energy Development (P046829)	China (EAP)	GEF	PV SHS	27,000,000	1,600,000	Closed (1,600,000)
11	Natural Gas Distribution for Low-Income Families in the Caribbean Coast (P102095)	Colombia (LAC)	GPOBA	Household gas connection and a gas stove	5,085,000	210,000[f]	Closed (210,000)[g]
12	Rural Energy Access (P105651)	Ethiopia (AFR)	GPOBA	Household connections	8,000,000	1,142,857	Implementation
13	Solar PV Systems to Increase Access to Electricity Services (P105617)	Ghana (AFR)	GPOBA	SHS installations	4,350,000	90,000	Implementation
14	Rural Electrification Plan (MIGA guarantee)	Guatemala (LAC)	MIGA	Individual household connections	[h]	1,100,000	Implementation (946,915)
15	Improved Electricity Access for Indian Slum Dwellers (P104649)	India (SAR)	GPOBA	Household connections	1,570,000	110,000	Design
16	Home Solar Systems (P035544)	Indonesia (EAP)	GEF	SHS installations	5,200,000	35,438	Closed
17	Southern Provinces Rural Electrification (P044973)	Lao PDR (EAP)	IDA	Household connections	1,000,000	50,000	Closed (51,805)
18	Electricity Access (P110723)	Liberia (AFR)	GPOBA	Household connections	5,000,000	91,241	Design
19	Household Energy and Universal Access (P073036)	Mali (AFR)	IDA, GEF	Household connections and SHS installations	19,300,000	178,700	Implementation (178,685)
20	Biogas Support Programme (P103979)	Nepal (SAR)	DGIS, KfW, GPOBA	Biogas plants	5,000,000	261,000	Implementation (64,840)[g]

(continued)

Project name (PO number)	Country or region	Funding source	Type of output	World Bank subsidy amount including GPOBA[a] (US$)	Planned number of beneficiaries	Project status (latest information on actual number of beneficiaries[b])
21 Offgrid Rural Electrification (PERZA) (P073246)	Nicaragua (LAC)	IDA	Household connections	1,850,000	42,000	Implementation (46,445)
22 Rural Power (P066397)	Philippines (EAP)	GEF	SHS installations	1,800,000	50,000	Implementation
23 Rural non-Grid Power Supply (P090238)	Philippines (EAP)	Local government technical assistance from GPOBA	Electricity supplied (kWh)	n.a.	360,000	Implementation
24 Electricity Services for Rural Areas (P085708)	Senegal (AFR)	IDA, GEF, AfDB, KfW	Household connections	18,000,000	377,622	Implementation
25 Renewable Energy for Rural Economic Development (P076702)	Sri Lanka (SAR)	GEF	SHS installations	3,900,000	425,000	Implementation (500,000)
26 Energy Services Delivery (P010498)	Sri Lanka (SAR)	IDA	SHS installations	5,700,000	75,000	Closed (104,765)
27 Pamir Private Power (P075256)	Tajikistan (ECA)	IDA	Electricity consumed (kWh)	4,000,000	178,126	Implementation (178,126)
28 Energy Development and Access (P101645)	Tanzania (AFR)	GEF	Rural household connections	2,300,000	75,000	Implementation
29 Energy for Rural Transformation Phase I (P069996)	Uganda (AFR)	GEF	SHS installations and institutional systems	1,400,000	37,500	Implementation (18,330)
30 Energy for Rural Transformation Phase II (P120108)	Uganda (AFR)	GPOBA	Household connections	10,000,000	1,060,000	Design

Water and sanitation

#	Project	Country (region)	Funding	Type			Status
1	Social Investment Program (P053578)	Bangladesh (SAR)	IDA	Water connections	314,743	26,000	Implementation (5,510)
2	Design of Innovative OBD Schemes for Water Supply and Sanitation Projects in Two Brazilian States (P114151)	Brazil (LAC)	TBC	Water and sanitation connections	TBC	TBC	Design
3	Water Affermage—OBA for Coverage Expansion (P106794)	Cameroon (AFR)	GPOBA	Water and sanitation connections	5,250,000	240,000	Implementation (24,000)[9]
4	Second Water Supply (P001044)	Guinea (AFR)	IDA	Water connections	16,900,000	138,000	Closed (138,000)
5	Extension of Water Services (P102474)	Honduras (LAC)	GPOBA	Water connections	4,440,000	240,000	Implementation
6	Improved Rural Community Water in Andhra Pradesh (P102472)	India (SAR)	GPOBA	Household water connections	850,000	75,000	Implementation (77,380)[9]
7	Jakarta PT Thames/Suez (P102529)	Indonesia (EAP)	GPOBA	Household water connections	2,573,140	55,824	Implementation (22,176)[9]
8	Expanding Piped Water Supply to Surabaya's Urban Poor (P105590)	Indonesia (EAP)	GPOBA	Water connections and master meter installation	2,407,500	77,500	Implementation
9	Microfinance for Water Services (P104075)	Kenya (AFR)	GPOBA, EU	Household water connections	1,151,300	60,000	Implementation (8,616)[9]
10	Extension of Water and Sanitation in Low-Income Areas in Kisumu (P098285)	Kenya (AFR)	GPOBA	Water connections	350,000	72,000	Design

(continued)

Project name (PO number)	Country or region	Funding source	Type of output	World Bank subsidy amount including GPOBA[a] (US$)	Planned number of beneficiaries	Project status (latest information on actual number of beneficiaries[b])
11 Small Towns Water Supply (P099575)	Lao PDR (EAP)	GPOBA	Water connections	2,350,000	124,000	Design
12 Guanajuato Water Project (TBC)	Mexico (LAC)	IBRD	Water and sanitation connections	38,006,000	90,640	Implementation
13 National OBA Facility for Wastewater Sector (P111610)	Mexico (LAC)	TBC	Water and sanitation connections	TBC	TBC	Design
14 Rural Water Supply and Sanitation (P086877)	Morocco (MENA)	Technical assistance from GPOBA	Water connections and flush latrines	N/A	51,840	Design
15 Urban Water and Sanitation (P102527)	Morocco (MENA)	GPOBA	Water and sanitation connections	7,000,000	55,704	Implementation (19,285)[9]
16 Water Private Sector Contracts—OBA for Coverage Expansion (P104945)	Mozambique (AFR)	GPOBA	Household yard taps	6,000,000	468,000	Implementation
17 Second National Urban Water Sector Reform (P071391)	Nigeria (AFR)	IDA	Household water connections	13,350,000	300,000	Implementation
18 Fourth Rural Water Supply and Sanitation (P039983)	Paraguay (LAC)	IBRD	Household water connections	834,880	27,625	Closed
19 National Project for Rural Water and Sanitation (P065256)	Peru (LAC)	IBRD	Household water connections	2,500,000	TBC	Implementation
20 LGU Urban Water and Sanitation Project APL2 (P069491)	Philippines (EAP)	IBRD	Household water connections	2,300,000	TBC	Closed

#	Project	Country (region)	Program	Indicator			Status
21	Manila Water Supply (P106775)	Philippines (EAP)	GPOBA	Water connections	2,900,000	100,463	Implementation (50,024)[9]
22	On-Site Water and Sanitation Project (P095587)	Senegal (AFR)	GPOBA	DP, septic tank, TCM, BALP	5,764,032	135,900	Implementation (9,801)[9]
23	On-Site Sanitation Project (IDA Project) (P041528)	Senegal (AFR)	IDA	Household sanitation connections	28,000,000	540,000	Implementation (567,000)
24	Colombo Wastewater (P111161)	Sri Lanka (SAR)	GPOBA	Sewer connections	1,100,000	35,000	Design
25	National Water Sector Fund (P104335)	St. Lucia (LAC)	GPOBA	Water connections	1,600,000	25,600	Design
26	Water Supply in Secondary Towns (P097290)	Tanzania (AFR)	GPOBA	Household water connections	7,000,000	100,000	Design
27	Water Supply in Uganda's Small Towns and Rural Growth Centers (P102462)	Uganda (AFR)	GPOBA	Public water points and household yard taps	3,169,001	55,511	Implementation (9,936)[9]
28	Kampala Water Connections for the Poor (P104943)	Uganda (AFR)	GPOBA	Public water points and yard taps	2,527,100	409,050	Implementation (31,785)
29	Rural Water (East Meets West) (P104528)	Vietnam (EAP)	GPOBA	Working house connection to network	3,000,000	150,000	Implementation (43,793)
30	Service Expansion and Water Loss Reduction (P106450)	Vietnam (EAP)	GPOBA	Individual household water connections	7,745,000	249,561	Implementation
31	Al Qabel Village Water Supply (P111757)	Yemen (MENA)	GPOBA	Household water connections	1,400,000	15,000	Design

(continued)

Project name (PO number)	Country or region	Funding source	Type of output	World Bank subsidy amount including GPOBA[a] (US$)	Planned number of beneficiaries	Project status (latest information on actual number of beneficiaries[b]
Health						
1 Health Sector Emergency Reconstruction and Development—Supplement (P098358)	Afghanistan (SAR)	IDA	Medical treatments	30,000,000	2,250,000	Implementation
2 Provincial Maternal-Child Health Investment Phase I (P071025)	Argentina (LAC)	IBRD, national government	Medical treatments for mothers and children	90,400,000	582,292	Closed (527,305)
3 Provincial Maternal-Child Health Investment Phase II (P095515)	Argentina (LAC)	IBRD, national government	Medical treatments for mothers and children	277,400,000	1,700,000	Implementation (388,188)
4 Contractual Approaches for Improving Health Services Delivery (P088751)	Congo, Dem. Rep. of (AFR)	IDA	Medical treatments	5,000,000	1,500,000	Implementation
5 Health Zone Project: Health Zone Administration and Facilities Contracting Component (P057296)	Congo, Dem. Rep. of (AFR)	IDA	Immunization coverage	5,000,000	10,000,000	Implementation
6 Rajasthan Health Systems Development (P050655)	India (SAR)	IDA, national government	Medical treatments	89,000,000	3,034,000	Implementation

#	Project	Country (region)	Funding	Treatment			Status
7	Lesotho New Hospital PPP (P104403)	Lesotho (AFR)	GPOBA	Medical treatments	6,250,000	500,000	Implementation
8	Prepaid Health Scheme Pilot (P104405)	Nigeria (AFR)	GPOBA	Medical treatments	6,015,165	22,500	Implementation
9	Poverty Reduction Support Credit (P078806)	Pakistan (SAR)	IDA	Medical treatments	TBC	TBC	Closed
10	Poverty Reduction Support Credit II (P090690)	Pakistan (SAR)	IDA	Medical treatments	TBC	TBC	Closed
11	Mother and Child Basic Health Insurance Project (P082056)	Paraguay (LAC)	IBRD	Mother-baby treatment package	7,304,000	737,000	Implementation
12	Phillippines Reproductive Health (P115184)	Philippines (EAP)	GPOEA	Mother-baby treatment package and reproductive health treatment	4,000,000	100,000	Design
13	Comparison of OBA Health Schemes (P092944)	Rwanda (AFR)	IDA, national government	Medical treatments	3,600,000	1,070,000	Closed
14	Poverty Reduction Support Credit I (P085192)	Rwanda (AFR)	IDA, national government	Medical treatments	13,000,000	TBC	Closed
15	Poverty Reduction Support Credit III (P098129)	Rwanda (AFR)	IDA, national government	Medical treatments	8,250,000	TBC	Closed
16	Poverty Reduction Support Credit IV (P104990)	Rwanda (AFR)	IDA, national government	Medical treatments	8,400,000	TBC	Closed
17	Health Sector Development (P058627)	Tanzania AFR	IDA	Medical treatments for maternal and childhood illnesses	267,486,000	TBC	Closed

(continued)

Project name (PO number)	Country or region	Funding source	Type of output	World Bank subsidy amount including GPOBA[a] (US$)	Planned number of beneficiaries	Project status (latest information on actual number of beneficiaries[b])
18 Health Sector Development II (P105093)	Tanzania (AFR)	IDA	Medical treatments to prevent Malaria	65,000,000	TBC	Implementation
19 Reproductive Health Vouchers in Western Uganda (P104527)	Uganda (AFR)	GPOBA, KfW	STD and safe delivery vouchers	4,300,000	135,912	Implementation (1,848)[i]
20 Mekong Regional Health Support (P079663)	Vietnam (EAP)	IDA	Health Insurance	8,000,000	TBC	Implementation
21 Health Support to the Poor of the Northern Upland (P110251)	Vietnam (EAP)	IDA	Medical treatments	14,140,000	TBC	Implementation
22 Safe Motherhood Program (P104946)	Yemen (MENA)	GPOBA	Mother-baby treatment package	6,232,100	80,000	Implementation (273)
Education						
1 Female Secondary School Assistance Project I (P009555)	Bangladesh (SAR)	IDA, national government	Female students enrolled	68,100,000	1,600,000	Closed (1,540,000)
2 Female Secondary School Assistance Project II (P044876)	Bangladesh (SAR)	IDA, national government	Female students enrolled	67,807,143	1,450,000	Closed (1,200,000)
3 Lifelong Learning and Training (P068271)	Chile (LAC)	IBRD, national government	Students enrolled	41,140,000	177,874	Implementation

| 4 | Balochistan Education Support (P094086) | Pakistan (SAR) | IDA, national government | Students enrolled | 2,100,000 | 34,500 | Implementation |
| 5 | Vietnam Education (P118797) | Vietnam (EAP) | GPOBA | Students enrolled | 3,000,000 | 10,000 | Design |

Notes: ADB = Asian Development Bank; AfDB = African Development Bank; AFR = Sub-Saharan Africa Region; BALP = bacs à laver puisards; DGIS = Netherlands Directorate-General for International Cooperation; DP = ; EAP = East Asia and Pacific Region; ECA = Europe and Central Asia Region; EU = European Union; GEF = Global Environment Facility; GPOBA = Global Partnership on Output-Based Aid; GTZ = German Agency for Technical Cooperation; IADB = Inter-American Development Bank; IBRD = International Bank for Reconstruction and Development; ICT = information and communication technology; IDA = International Development Association; IDB = Islamic Development Bank; IDCOL = Infrastructure Development Company Limited; IXP = Internet exchange point; KfW = Kreditanstalt für Wiederaufbau; km = kilometer; kWh = kilowatt-hour; LAC = Latin America and Caribbean Region; MENA = Middle East and North Africa Region; MIGA = Multilateral Investment Guarantee Agency; NDF = Nordic Development Fund; OBA = output-based aid; PO = purchase order; PoP = point of presence; PV = photovoltaic; SAR = South Asia Region; SHS = solar home system; STD = sexually transmitted disease; TBC = to be confirmed; TCM = toilette à chasse manuelle.

a. This amount does not include any government subsidy contribution, which totals nearly US$1.7 billion.

b. The latest information on the actual number of beneficiaries is available only for projects that have received either technical assistance or investment subsidy funding from GPOBA or both, as well as for a few other World Bank Group projects.

c. According to the implementation completion reports, the OBA component of the project was cancelled in June 2008. The operator failed to meet the technical specifications and comply with the deadlines for installation of the telecenters. The project had paid US$1.00 million of the US$4.15 million committed as advances and for the reported installation of half the telecenters. None of the telecenters is in operation.

d. For Mongolia Telecom, the number of final beneficiaries increased because of competitive bidding.

e. In effect, from 1998 to 2005, about 4,000 kilometers (km) of rehabilitation works on the federal road network were undertaken with World Bank funding, and about 3,500 km of those works were done with a result-based approach. An additional 3,000 km of rehabilitation works were financed by Inter-American Development Bank loans, and about 1,300 km by the federal government itself.

f. The verified connections in Colombia serve 204,852 beneficiaries. The remaining 5,000 beneficiaries were connected, but the connections were not verified because they were made after the deadline.

g. This includes beneficiaries from unverified connections.

h. The World Bank Group contributed to this project in the form of a Multilateral Investment Guarantee Agency guarantee, providing insurance coverage for the privatization of two state-run power distribution companies in Guatemala (Distribuidora Electrica de Oriente S.A. and Distribuidora Electrica de Occidente S.A.). The US$96.6 million guarantee was extended to Union Fenosa Internacional S.A, of Spain, to protect the investment against the risks of transfer restriction, expropriation, and war and civil disturbance. In addition to assuming management and operational control, the privatization was part of Guatemala's rural electrification framework.

i. This number refers to the 1,356 pre-natal care visits received by mothers and 246 safe deliveries (two beneficiaries per safe delivery).

j. To be confirmed.

k. Not available.

References

ADB (Asian Development Bank). 2003. *Road Funds and Road Maintenance: An Asian Perspective*. Manila, Philippines: Asian Development Bank.

Africa News Update, The Norwegian Council for Africa. 2007. "Uganda: Employers Reject Health Insurance Scheme." http://www.afrika.no/Detailed/14807.html.

Baker, Bill, and Sophie Tremolet. 2000. "Regulating Quality: Let Competing Firms Offer a Mix of Price and Quality Options." Private Policy for the Private Sector, note 221. World Bank, Washington, DC. http://rru.worldbank.org/Documents/PublicPolicyJournal/221Baker-10-24.pdf.

Bardasi, Elena, and Quentin Wodon. 2008. "Who Pays the Most for Water? Alternative Providers and Service Costs in Niger." *Economics Bulletin* 9 (20): 1–10.

Barrera-Osorio, Felipe. 2006. "The Impact of Private Provision of Public Education: Empirical Evidence from Bogotá's Concession Schools." Policy Research Working Paper 4121, World Bank, Washington, DC. http://econ.worldbank.org/external/default/main?pagePK=64165259&theSitePK=469372&piPK=64165421&menuPK=64166322&entityID=000016406_20070126111542.

Birdsall, Nancy, William D. Savedoff, Katherine Vyborny, and Ayah Mahgoub. 2008. "Cash on Delivery Aid: A New Approach to Foreign Aid Applied to Primary Schooling." Center for Global Development, Washington, DC.

Booth, Kathleen L. S. 2006. *New Approaches to PPP in the Roads Sector: India's Annuity Concessions.* Washington, DC: Institute for Public-Private Partnerships.

Brook, Penelope J., and Murray Petrie. 2001. "Output-Based Aid: Precedents, Promises, and Challenges." In *Contracting for Public Services: Output-Based Aid and Its Applications,* ed. Penelope J. Brook and Suzanne M. Smith, 3–11. Washington, DC: World Bank.

Brown, David. 2008. "Number of Children Immunized Has Been Inflated for Years." *Washington Post,* December 12: A03.

Cabana, Guillermo, Gerard Liautaud, and Asif Faiz. 1999. "Areawide Performance-Based Rehabilitation and Maintenance Contracts for Low-Volume Roads." Presentation to the Seventh International Conference on Low-Volume Roads, May 23–27. http://siteresources.worldbank.org/INTROADSHIGHWAYS/Resources/338993-1122496826968/7thiclv.pdf.

de Gouvello, Christophe, and Geeta Kumar. 2007. "OBA in Senegal—Designing Technology-Neutral Concessions for Rural Electrification." *OBApproaches,* note 14. Global Partnership on Output-Based Aid, Washington, DC.

Dymond, Andrew, Sonja Oestmann, and Scott McConnell. 2008. "Output-Based Aid in Mongolia: Expanding Telecommunications Services to Rural Areas." *OBApproaches,* note 18. Global Partnership on Output-Based Aid, Washington, DC.

Flyvbjerg, Bent. 2005. "Policy and Planning for Large Infrastructure Projects: Problems, Causes, Cures." Policy Research Working Paper 3781, World Bank, Washington, DC.

Flyvbjerg, Bent, Mette Skamris Holm, and Soren Buhl. 2002. "Underestimating Costs in Public Works Projects: Error or Lie." *Journal of the American Planning Association* 68 (3): 279–95.

Gassner, Katharina, Alexander Popov, and Nataliya Pushak. 2007. "An Empirical Assessment of Private Sector Participation in Electricity and Water Distribution in Developing and Transition Countries." Public-Private Infrastructure Advisory Facility, Washington, DC.

Gómez-Lobo, Andrés. 2001. "Making Water Affordable: Output-Based Consumption Subsidies in Chile." In *Contracting for Public Services: Output-Based Aid and Its Applications,* ed. Penelope J. Brook and Suzanne M. Smith, 23–30. Washington, DC: World Bank.

Grosch, Margaret, Carlo del Ninno, Emil Tesliuc, and Azedine Ouerghi. 2008. "For Protection and Promotion: The Design and Implementation of Effective Safety Nets." Washington, DC: World Bank.

Harris, Clive. 2002. "Private Sector Power: Network Expansion Using an Output-Based Scheme in Guatemala." *World Bank Viewpoint, note* 245. World Bank, Washington, DC.

Hartwig, Tim, Yogita Mumssen, and Andreas Schliessler. 2005. "Output-Based Aid in Chad: Using Performance-Based Contracts to Improve Roads." *OBApproaches*, note 6. Global Partnership on Output-Based Aid, Washington, DC.

Johannes, Lars, Patrick Mullen, Peter Okwero, and Miriam Schneidman. 2008. "Performance-Based Contracting in Health: The Experience of Three Projects in Africa." *OBApproaches*, note 19. Global Partnership on Output-Based Aid, Washington, DC.

Komives, Kristin, Vivien Foster, Jonathan Halpern, and Quentin Wodon, with support from Roohi Abdullah. 2005. *Water, Electricity, and the Poor: Who Benefits from Utility Subsidies?* Washington, DC: World Bank.

Lemaire, Xavier. 2007. "Case Study: Concession for Rural Electrification with Solar Home Systems in Kwazulu-Natal (South Africa)." Centre for Management under Regulation, Warwick Business School, United Kingdom.

Liautaud, Girard. 2001. "Maintaining Roads: The Argentine Experience with Output-Based Contracts." *Public Policy for the Private Sector*, note 231. http://rru.worldbank.org/documents/publicpolicyjournal/231Liaut-531.pdf.

Lim, Stephen S., David B. Stein, Alexandra Charrow, and Christopher J. L. Murray. 2008. "Tracking Progress towards Universal Childhood Immunisation and the Impact of Global Initiatives: A Systematic Analysis of Three-Dose Diphtheria, Tetanus, and Pertussis Immunisation Coverage." *Lancet* 372 (9655): 2031–2046.

Mandri-Perrott, Cledan. 2008. "Output-Based Aid in India: Community Water Project in Andhra Pradesh." *OBApproaches*, note 21. Global Partnership on Output-Based Aid, Washington, DC.

Mumssen Yogita, and Kenny Charles. 2007. OBA in Infrastructure: A Tool for Reducing the Impact of Corruption. http://www.gpoba.org/gpoba/sites/gpoba.org/files/OBApproaches16_CorruptionOBA.pdf.

National Highway Maintenance Contract Seminar. 2005. *Highway Maintenance Contracting 2004, World State of Practices: Report of the National Highway Maintenance Contract Seminar, April 2004, Orlando, Florida*. Washington, DC: U.S. Department of Transportation, Federal Highway Administration.

Navarro, Mariles, and Luiz Tavares. 2008. "Output-Based Aid in Cambodia: Getting Private Operators and Local Communities to Help Deliver Water to the Poor—the Experience to Date." OBA Working Paper Series, Paper no. 9, Global Partnership on Output-Based Aid, Washington, DC.

Navas-Sabater, Juan, and Mavis Ampah. 2007. "Output-Based Aid in Uganda: Bringing Communications Services to Rural Areas." *OBApproaches*, note 15. Global Partnership on Output-Based Aid, Washington, DC.

Ramatlapeng, Mphu K. 2007. "Public Private Partnership for Replacing the National Referral Hospital." PowerPoint presentation by the Minister of Health and Social Welfare, Lesotho, to the Health, Nutrition and Population Learning Program, World Bank, Washington, DC, October 3.

Reiche, Kilian, Alvaro Covarrubias, and Eric Martinot. 2000. "Expanding Electricity Access to Remote Areas: Off-Grid Rural Electrification in Developing Countries." http://www.martinot.info/Reiche_et_al_WP2000.pdf.

Reiche, Kilian, Dana Rysankova, and Sue Goldmark. 2006. "Output-Based Subsidies for Access: Early Lessons for Practitioners from Three Recent Off-grid Electrification Projects in Latin America." ESMAP Report, World Bank, Washington, DC.

Segal, Geoffrey F., Adrian T. Moore, and Samuel McCarthy. 2003. "Contracting for Road and Highway Maintenance." Reason Foundation, Los Angeles, California.

Stankevich, Natalya, Navaid Qureshi, and Cesar Queiroz. 2005 (updated 2009). "Performance-Based Contracting for Preservation and Improvement of Road Assets." Transport note TN-27, World Bank, Washington, DC.

Stern, Peter, and David Townsend. 2007. *New Models for Universal Access to Telecommunications Services in Latin America: Lessons from the Past and Recommendations for a New Generation of Universal Access Programs for the 21st Century.* Report for the Forum of Latin American Telecommunications Regulators (Regulatel), the World Bank through its trust funds PPIAF and GPOBA, the European Commission, and the Economic Commission for Latin America (ECLAC).

Terrado, Ernesto, Anil Cabraal, and Ishani Mukherjee. 2008. "Operational Guidance for World Bank Group Staff: Designing Sustainable Off-Grid Rural Electrification Projects: Principles and Practices." World Bank, Energy and Mining Sector Board, Washington, DC.

UNDP (United Nations Development Programme). 2006. *Human Development Report 2006: Beyond Scarcity: Power, Poverty and the Global Water Crisis.* New York: Palgrave Macmillan. http://hdr.undp.org/en/reports/global/hdr2006/.

Virjee, Kameel. 2009. "Leveraging Private Sector Finance for Rural Piped Water Infrastructure in Kenya: The Use of Output-Based Aid." *OBApproaches,* note 30. Global Partnership on Output-Based Aid, Washington, DC.

Wellenius, Björn. 2002. "Closing the Gap in Access to Rural Communications: Chile 1995–2002." World Bank Discussion Paper 430, World Bank, Washington, DC.

World Bank. 1994. "Executive Summary." In *World Development Report 1994: Infrastructure for Development.* Washington, DC: World Bank. http://www-wds.worldbank.org/external/default/WDSContentServer/IW3P/IB/2007/10/10/0 00011823_20071010172019/Rendered/PDF/13483.pdf.

———. 2009. Project appraisal document for Uganda-Second energy for Rural Transformation (ERT II) Project. http://projportal.worldbank.org/servlet/secmain?pagePK=219321&piPK=219326&theSitePK=213348&conceptattcode=UG-Uganda%3A+Energy+For+Rural+Transformation+Apl-2+--+P112334~998365|Project%20Appraisal%20Document~540656&PSPID=P112334&menuPK=109012.

———. 2002. "Renewable Energy for Rural Economic Development." Project appraisal document for Sri Lanka Rural Electrification and Renewable Energy Development Project. http://web.worldbank.org/external/projects/main?pagePK=64283627&piPK=73230&theSitePK=40941&menuPK=228424&Projectid=P076702.

———. 2003. *World Development Report 2004: Making Services Work for Poor People*. Washington, DC: World Bank and Oxford University Press.

———. 2005a. "Bangladesh: Solar Home Program on Credit Sales." http://siteresources.worldbank.org/EXTRENENERGYTK/Resources/5138246-1238175210723/Bangladesh0Sol1ram0on0Credit0Sales0.pdf.

———. 2005b. "The Democratic Republic of Congo Health Sector Rehabilitation Support Project." Project Information Document P088751. http://web.worldbank.org/external/projects/main?pagePK=64283627&piPK=73230&theSitePK=40941&menuPK=228424&Projectid=P088751.

———. 2006a. "Health Sector Emergency Reconstruction and Development Project (Supplement)." Project Information Document P098358. http://web.worldbank.org/external/projects/main?pagePK=64312881&piPK=64302848&theSitePK=40941&Projectid=P098358.

———. 2006b. "Implementation Completion Report of National Highways Rehabilitation and Maintenance Project in Argentina." http://www-wds.worldbank.org/external/default/main?pagePK=64193027&piPK=64187937&theSitePK=523679&menuPK=64187510&searchMenuPK=64187283&siteName=WDS&entityID=000160016_20060629105649.

———. 2007a. "The Country-Based Development Model and Scaling Up." Scaling Up Newsletter Series, PREM Poverty Reduction Group Number 2, World Bank, Washington, DC.

———. 2007b. *Healthy Development: The World Bank's Strategy for Health, Nutrition, and Population Results*. Washington, DC: World Bank.

———. 2007c. "Lesotho New Hospital PPP." Project Information Document P104403. http://web.worldbank.org/external/projects/main?pagePK=64283627&piPK=73230&theSitePK=40941&menuPK=228424&Projectid=P104403.

———. 2008a. "Argentina: $50 Million for Green Energy in Rural Areas." Press Release 2009/137/LRC, World Bank, Washington, DC. http://web.worldbank

.org/WBSITE/EXTERNAL/NEWS/0,,contentMDK:21974682~menuPK: 34467~pagePK:34370~piPK:34424~theSitePK:4607,00.html.

———. 2008b. *Issues Note of the REToolkit: A Resource for Renewable Energy Development*, June 30, 2008. Washington, DC: World Bank.

———. 2008c. "Norway Provides US$105 Million to World Bank for Better Health Results in Poor Countries." News Release 2008/123/HDN, World Bank, Washington, DC. http://go.worldbank.org/04UNXY1MS0.

———. 2008d. "Procurement Issues in Structuring Output-Based Aid (OBA) Operations Financed by the World Bank: Guidance Note for Procurement Staff," April 11, 2008. World Bank, Washington, DC. http://www.gpoba.org/ gpoba/sites/gpoba.org/files/GuidanceNote.PR_.OBA_.pdf.

———. 2009a. *2009 Annual Review of Development Effectiveness: Achieving Sustainable Development.* Independent Evaluation Group Studies. Washington, DC: World Bank.

———. 2009b. "Implementation Completion Report of Natural Gas Distribution for Low Income Families in the Caribbean Coast Project." http://projportal .worldbank.org/servlet/secmain?menuPK=109012&theSitePK=213348& piPK=69345&pagePK=112935&PSPID=P102095.

———. 2009c. "Investment Lending Reform: Concept Note." Operations Policy and Country Services, World Bank, Washington DC.

———. 2009d. *Performance-Based Contracting for Preservation and Improvement of Road Assets: Resource Guide.* Washington, DC: World Bank. http://www-esd .worldbank.org/pbc_resource_guide/index.html.

———. 2009e. *Toolkit for Public-Private Partnerships in Roads and Highways.* 2nd ed. http://rru.worldbank.org/Toolkits/PartnershipsHighways/.

———. 2009f. "World Bank–International Finance Corporation Collaboration in IDA Countries: A Progress Report." IDA-IFC Secretariat, Washington, DC.

Zietlow, Gunter. 2004. "Implementing Performance-Based Road Management and Maintenance Contracts in Developing Countries: An Instrument of German Technical Co-operation." German Technical Cooperation, Eschborn.

Index

Boxes, figures, notes, and tables are indicated by *b*, *f*, *n*, and *t*, respectively.

www.ingramcontent.com/pod-product-compliance
Lightning Source LLC
Chambersburg PA
CBHW070916270326
41927CB00011B/2592